WOMEN IN THE MIDDLE AGES

GEMMA HOLLMAN

WOMEN IN THE MIDDLE AGES

ILLUMINATING THE WORLD
OF PEASANTS, NUNS, AND QUEENS

Abbeville Press
Novum Eboracum · Londinium

To Conor, for everything. —Gemma Hollman

ABOUT THE AUTHOR

Gemma Hollman is a historian and author of *The Queen and the Mistress: The Women of Edward III* and *Royal Witches: Witchcraft and the Nobility in Fifteenth-Century England*. A Fellow of the Royal Historical Society, she works full-time in the heritage industry while running her historical blog, *Just History Posts*.

Front cover: Illustration details from the Codex Manesse, fol. 204r (*top left*); fol. 52r (*top right*; see page 109); fol. 32v (*bottom left*); fol. 98r (*bottom center*); fol. 63r (*bottom right*). Switzerland, 1300–1340. Heidelberg University Library, Germany; Cod. Pal. germ. 848.
Back cover: *Window of Saint Catherine*, northern Netherlands, c. 1475. See page 68.
Pages 2–3: Master of the Cité des Dames (active 1400–1415). Christine de Pisan, *The Book of the City of Ladies* (detail), fol. 2r. See page 41.

EDITOR: Lauren Orthey
COPY EDITOR: Amy K. Hughes
INDEXER: Tobiah Waldron
DESIGN: Misha Beletsky and Marina Drukman
PRODUCTION DIRECTOR: Louise Kurtz

First edition
10 9 8 7 6 5 4 3 2 1

Library of Congress Cataloging-in-Publication Data
Names: Hollman, Gemma, author.
Title: Women in the Middle Ages: illuminating the world of peasants, nuns, and queens / Gemma Hollman.
Description: First edition. | New York: Abbeville Press, [2024] | Includes bibliographical references and index. |
Summary: "An illustrated book that uses art to illuminate the lives of medieval women"—Provided by publisher.
Identifiers: LCCN 2024031744 | ISBN 9780789214966 (hardcover)
Subjects: LCSH: Women—Europe—History—Middle Ages, 500–1500. | Women—Europe—Social conditions. | Women in art.
Classification: LCC HQ1147.E85 H65 2024 | DDC 305.409401—dc23/eng/20240716
LC record available at https://lccn.loc.gov/2024031744

For bulk and premium sales and for text adoption procedures, write to Customer Service Manager, Abbeville Press, 655 Third Avenue, New York, NY 10017, or call 1-800-ARTBOOK.

Visit Abbeville Press online at www.abbeville.com.

CONTENTS

THE WORLD OF MEDIEVAL WOMEN

Women have been part of humanity since the beginning of time. But if you picked up many history books, you would not always be aware of this fact. For centuries, male historians in Europe wrote histories of other men and their business, with women often appearing as footnotes when their presence could not quite be ignored. Over the past two hundred years, though, this began to change. On the cusp of the Victorian era in England, the Strickland sisters entered the scene and began to steer the narrative away from "Great Men and Their Deeds" to look instead at great women. Elizabeth and Agnes Strickland researched every queen of England and published a fantastic twelve-volume series that is still important today (if, rather sadly, because many of these queens still have not received further attention).

Historians across Europe slowly began to turn their attention to famous women from history and then, after that, to their more "ordinary" counterparts. Even today, women's history is a relatively young field, and there remains so much more work to do to peel back the hidden stories of the women who came before us. Part of the historian's problem is the difficulty in accessing sources that talk about these women. For much of the Middle Ages, the literate people who were recording what was happening around them were men. They, in turn, were writing about the men around them: the kings, the nobles, the statesmen, the churchmen, the soldiers. Even official records document men over and over because they were the ones in governmental positions. Women do turn up, but they are usually high-status women who had the privilege of being at court or running their own noble estates.

So, where does one turn to find the ordinary woman? And how much can we really know about the life of a woman in medieval Europe? One place to begin our search is, perhaps surprisingly, in art. We are used to beautiful women being used as models in paintings in later periods, but in the Middle Ages women appeared in countless pieces of art in everyday life. The walls of cold stone castles were draped with elaborate tapestries depicting a plethora of scenes; churches were a kaleidoscope of colors depicting biblical teachings to a largely illiterate population, and those who could read possessed manuscripts littered with drawings. Even official documents were soon adorned by the doodles of bored scribes. Nuns, artists, scholars, housewives, and royalty are all depicted, and as the artists wanted to portray the reality around them, these artworks

↑ This vase or drug jar has a portrait of a woman, possibly Eleanor of Aragon.

Vase or drug jar, Italy (Naples), c. 1475
Painted tin-glazed earthenware, height: 13½ in. (34.5 cm)
Victoria and Albert Museum, London

←← *Love Story in Pictures*, fol. 4v, France (Touraine), early 16th century
Detail of page 121

↑ Maria Ormani was an Italian nun who copied and illustrated a breviary (liturgical book) in 1453. She left us a beautiful self-portrait with her name in a scroll around the edges at the bottom of one of the pages.

Maria Ormani (1428–c. 1470)
Breviary (detail), fol. 89r, Italy, 1453
Österreichische Nationalbibliothek, Vienna; Cod. 1923

→ As the medieval period progressed, artists found more work, and style developed. Casual sketches that were either practice or templates for more formal portraits survive in abundance and can provide us with beautiful snapshots of contemporary women. This sketch shows two Dutch women wearing different styles of headdresses.

Two Women's Heads, 1400–1500
Pen and ink, 4 × 6 in. (10 × 15 cm)
Rijksmuseum, Amsterdam;
RP-T-1947-25

can be fantastic sources for social history. The changing fashions of different centuries, the tools used by peasants, and subtle social commentaries can all enrich our knowledge of women at this time. Many women even placed themselves in the art they created, leaving tiny self-portraits that survive today.

This book looks to scrape the surface of centuries of history across Europe to reveal a glimpse into what life was like for women in a time traditionally thought to have been repressive. Modern depictions of medieval life, including those drawn upon for popular fantasy series, often show it as gray, dire, and bleak, and certainly not a time to want to be a woman. Women tend to be portrayed as victims of a vicious patriarchy that valued them solely for their lands and beauty, abused and powerless, but this is not the full story. True, some women did suffer horrendous fates at this time, and it certainly was not an equal society. But women were far more valued than many realize, and most were able to have a voice in the decisions of their lives.

Most women in society were not wealthy enough to be mere adornments to men and had to work for a living, but even those of higher classes needed to work hard to manage estates or religious institutions—or even kingdoms. While we may think medieval women could choose only to be a wife or a nun, there were plenty

→ Women were found on all kinds of art in the Middle Ages, including on jewelry. This brooch depicts a pair of aristocratic lovers standing in a garden underneath a tree. It would have been a treasured item for its use of enamel, a fairly new technique at the time.

Brooch with lovers, Burgundian or Netherlands, 1430–40
Gold, enamel, pearls, precious stones, diameter: 2 in. (5 cm)
Kunsthistorisches Museum, Vienna

→→ A couple in a loving embrace decorates a page in an anthology of courtly poetry. Women were both the subjects and writers of such poetry.

Codex Manesse (detail), fol. 249v, Switzerland, 1300–1340
Heidelberg University Library, Germany; Cod. Pal. germ. 848

who carved out careers in industry and supported their families. There were women who worked hard to live up to the feminine ideal, while others fought against the expectations placed on them, leading armies into battle, as did Joan of Arc; writing tracts defending women and their virtues, like Christine de Pisan; and even ruling kingdoms in their own right, like Jadwiga of Poland.

Together, we will cover many different countries in Catholic Europe, roughly across the later medieval period, around AD 1000–1500. By its nature, this breadth of coverage means there will have to be generalizations in our journey, and what we explore at any one time will not be universal for all women in all these countries across all five hundred years. Although the countries we are looking at were under the sphere of Christendom, Jewish and Muslim women also lived in these regions and would have had different experiences, which will not be covered here. But by looking at the compelling visual material for the period and supplementing this with case studies of known women, we can get a taste of what it was like for some of these women of centuries ago. Let us explore the women of the Middle Ages: the peasants, the nuns, the scholars, the artists, and the aristocracy.

I. PEASANTS AND PROFESSIONALS

Medieval Europe was ruled by the Three Estates, the three groups into which society was neatly divided: the church, the nobles, and the commons. While Christendom was a patriarchy, women were present in all three estates. At the start of our period, the commons meant the peasants, but as the Middle Ages progressed, a new class began to spring up across Europe. Although it was not quite the "middle class" as we may consider it today, the growth in trade and skilled professionals led to a bourgeois class made up of reasonably wealthy—and powerful—merchants and craftspeople. As the medieval period drew to a close, those who inhabited this rank found themselves in significant positions of influence in urban centers across Europe, with access to royal courts opened up to them through their affluence. Though women in this rank did not gain political power as the men around them did, their lives were substantially different from those of their peasant sisters.

Regardless of their station, all women had to work. As we'll see, the world of work was open to peasant and professional women. What did it mean to be a medieval woman who earned a living? The first point to consider is how to define work. Throughout time, women's work has traditionally been ignored, minimized, and marginalized. Raising children, cooking, keeping a house clean, overseeing the family, supporting a husband, and growing food, while vital for the maintenance of society, were often (and still can be) not considered "real work." Many women in the medieval period were housewives whether they also worked for a salary or not. Though she and her contemporaries did not consider the role to be a "job," the medieval housewife's contribution to maintaining the family unit was still seen as vital. Women were the lifeblood of the home, and without them, how was a man to work and build his legacy?

The plethora of roles a woman was expected to perform did not go unacknowledged. *The Ballad of the Tyrannical Husband*, the tale of an angry man and his good wife, was composed in the late fifteenth century and survives in a single London merchant's book of texts. The grumpy husband came home one day from plowing and complained that his wife had not prepared dinner for him. He queries what she could possibly have spent her day doing, claiming she had nothing to do but sit at home or gossip with the neighbors. The indignant wife reels off a list of her tasks. Having been up all night caring for their children, she had risen before her husband, milked the cows, and turned them into the field. Across the course of the

The Blinding of Tobit, *Bible Historiale of Edward IV*, fol. 18r, southern Netherlands (Bruges), c. 1479
Detail of page 54

day, she proceeded to make butter and cheese, continued to care for the crying children, fed the chickens, ducks, and geese, then baked bread and brewed ale, before processing flax, spinning wool, and making clothes for the family. Eventually the couple make a wager, whereby the husband will be the housewife for a day while the wife goes out to plow. The end of the ballad is lost, but its composition certainly suggests that the wife succeeds in the field, while caring for the home ends disastrously for the husband.[1]

Peasants are usually depicted at work rather than in their homes, but pictures of the Holy Family can give us an insight into peasant life. The Virgin Mary and Joseph were of humble origins and are often shown as such in a domestic setting. In this charming picture, Mary suckles the Christ Child, and Joseph eats while sitting in a chair fashioned from a barrel. The room is small, with a pot over the fire, and its decor is simple—the plaster behind the fire is cracked and peeling.

Master of Catherine of Cleves (active c. 1435–1460)
Hours of Catherine of Cleves (detail), p. 151, Netherlands (Utrecht), c. 1440
Morgan Library and Museum, New York; MS M.917/945

Two women capture a rabbit from a warren by sending a stoat inside and laying a cage at the other exit.

Queen Mary Psalter (detail), fol. 155v, England, c. 1310–20
British Library, London; Royal 2 B VII

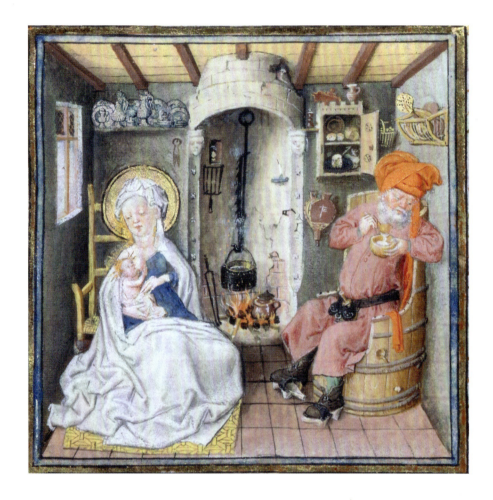

Being a housewife is hard today, and it was hard in the medieval period. Life was difficult, and household tasks were laborious and arduous, with limited technology to make them easier. It is important that we recognize this aspect of life for common women of the time. But the tasks that women were expected to carry out as wives and mothers were important in another sense, as they influenced what society deemed acceptable as work for women. As women moved into the world of work outside of the home, their career opportunities were directed by the work they already did within the home. The greatest opportunities, and the greatest respect, were found in professions that were an extension of the role of housewife: that of provider of food and textiles, of caregiver, and of household manager. This pattern is very much followed in the art of the period, as peasants and professionals are most often depicted working. While women can be seen occasionally performing tasks less common for their gender, most are shown farming, caring for animals and children, and working with textiles. Manuscript drawings, in particular, are a ripe place to find ordinary women; whereas individual holy or noble women sometimes had statues erected in their honor or were shown in shimmering stained glass windows or beautifully intricate tapestries, peasant women found a place in the doodles and marginalia that accompanied written pieces of the period. These images can provide us with great insight into how these women dressed and undertook their jobs and daily lives, bringing them to the foreground when the written records would otherwise ignore their presence.

RURAL WOMEN

As the year 1000 arrived, towns and cities existed in Europe, but urban centers were limited. There were a few blooming metropolises, and countries and states were still forming. While trade flourished, in many places in Europe it was limited in scope. Many people lived

The Ballad of the Tyrannical Husband revealed the never-ending list of tasks peasant women had to complete in a day. This woman is shown below feeding chickens while holding her distaff under her arm, ready to return to spinning thread once the animals have been cared for, balancing tasks just like the wife from the ballad.

Luttrell Psalter (detail), fol. 166v, England, 1320–40
British Library, London;
Add MS 42130

Medieval art sometimes poked fun at the amount of work a housewife had to undertake. Astride a donkey, this woman carries a baby, two ducks, and a cooking pot while spinning a distaff and herding animals. The text in the scroll reads, "I have plenty of household goods; otherwise I would not be so important."

The Wandering Housewife,
Switzerland, 1470–80
Wool and linen tapestry panel,
33⅞ × 42⅞ in. (86 × 109 cm)
Glasgow Museums, Scotland

rural, agricultural lives based on subsistence and serving their local lords. Women were central to this rural lifestyle, and they continued to be as the Middle Ages progressed.

Agriculture was defined by the environment, the weather, and the seasons. If you couldn't grow or trade goods somewhat locally, then you didn't obtain them unless you had the money and power to do so. Within the Three Estates system, feudalism and similar structures dominated in Europe. Peasants may have had their own small holdings, but they were not enough to live on and were often rented from their local lords. In order to make a living, peasants had to work their liege's lands and use their spare time to manage their own crops and animals. The physical labor of growing crops was grueling. The toil of pulling the plow alongside the oxen and swinging scythes to harvest the crops was largely reserved for men, but women still needed to participate wherever possible. They would weed the crops and tidy the fields during the growing season and help collect chaff, stalks, and kernels left behind by the men as they harvested.

Certain crops that required less strength to care for easily lent themselves to women's work. In Seville, a seasonal balance was found between men's and women's work. The majority of the region's peasants owned small farms planted with grapevines that could be managed most of the time by women. The large estates of the major landholders were given over to cereals and olives, which both sustained the region and gave it flourishing trade. During July and August, the cereals required harvesting, and this work was carried out exclusively by men in the region, who would leave their homes in large numbers to work for the estates. In September, the grapes had ripened on the vines of the peasants, who were now free to reap their own rewards.

Then, when November arrived, the olives of the great estates were ready for picking. Collecting the vast numbers of olives could last into the start of January, and while it was tiring, as it required working every day from dawn to dusk, it was not too physically demanding. For this harvest, the women of Seville traveled to the estates and spent the next few months living in specially built harvesters'

↙ Although women rarely did the most physical farm labor, they were required to help during every season. In this image, a woman waits with a rake to gather up the crops that the man has harvested with a scythe.

Pietro Crescenzi, *Ruralia Commoda* (Speyer, Germany: Peter Drach) (detail), page 221, 1490
Biblioteca Nazionale Centrale di Firenze, Italy

↓ The labors of the months was a popular motif in medieval artwork, depicting different tasks based on the season for each month of the year. Many of these labors involved peasants, and so these images provide insight into everyday life. This stained glass roundel shows the month of August, represented by a woman bending over to harvest grain with a sickle.

Labours of the Months (August), England, 1450–75
Stained glass panel, diameter: 8⅜ in. (21.5 cm)
Victoria and Albert Museum, London

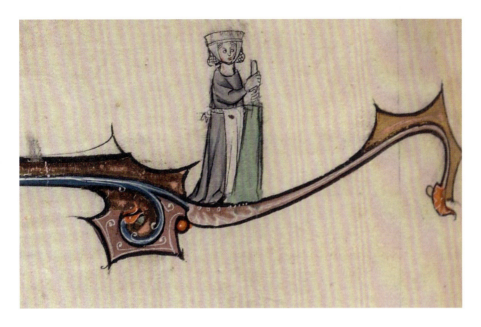

houses on the farms. Contracted to work by the basketful, they were known as *cogederas*, or "catchers." Women of all ages undertook this work, and they would have spent the sunlight hours toiling away. Many brought their children with them—not to supervise them as their mothers but because the children were active participants in the harvest even from as young as six years of age. The women's contracts for olive harvesting could be drawn up months in advance, with payment being made at the point of signing. Many families used these payments to stretch their money during the spring, when there was little work available, paying off the debt with their labor through the autumn and winter. While the women were away, the men would stay home and tend to their own vines, pruning and preparing them for winter.[2]

Many other European regions had seasonal cycles of labor divided between men and women. Generally, though, women's farmwork was multifaceted, and they were expected to react to the needs of the moment. While they had regular, daily jobs they needed to do, women were considered cheap, available labor to be on hand as and when needed, such as during harvest. Pastoral agriculture, or animal husbandry, is where women's labor was particularly focused. It was usually women who cared for animals, feeding and watering them, turning them into the fields, and collecting their produce, whether it be eggs, wool, milk, or feathers. They were also expected to undertake the initial processing of these products—churning milk into butter and cheese, spinning wool into thread, or cooking food for the family.

A common task for rural women was the brewing of ale. Despite pervasive myths, medieval people did not drink alcohol because it was safer than water—they generally had access to clean water sources, and alcohol was purely for enjoyment or nutrition. At times when the harvest was poor, the least wealthy members of society

would not have wasted their limited grains in brewing ale, but in normal years it was a common household task for women. To create ale, grains were soaked to release their sugars and then heated in a kiln. The concoction was then crushed and mixed with hot water in order to dissolve the sugars, and finally the liquid was filtered out from the rest of the mixture and left to ferment. Although its manufacture was a relatively simple process, ale did not preserve well and so had to be brewed regularly in small quantities. In most rural households, the women would have made ale a couple of times a month, the family consuming it as they went, but large households and religious centers may have had a more industrial-scale production line. In plentiful times, any extra ale produced by the housewife could always be sold for extra coin at market.[3]

Not all rural women were housewives; another significant proportion of women in rural Europe who had to engage in agriculture were religious women. As we will come to see, many nuns lived in rural communities sequestered away from busy urban centers so that they could focus their lives on prayer, removed from the sins of the common people. Despite this isolation, and although many nunneries had servants and agricultural workers to help provide for them, religious women across the Middle Ages got their hands dirty with this type of work too.

Although peasant women could be involved in any aspect of farm-work, it was considered unbecoming for religious women to engage

in the hardest areas of farm labor. But they did raise animals and grow crops seen as more suitable to women's work—particularly in vineyards. Nuns also became associated with caring for sheep, which provided not only food but also much-needed cloth to work with. These were not always small-scale farmholdings—the nuns at the Icelandic convent Kirkjubæjarklaustur kept more sheep not only than any other religious house in the country but even more than any farm in Iceland.[4]

While much of Europe was divided into private estates and peasant smallholdings, there were also swaths of common land, which any member of society could make use of to supplement their living. This land could be used to graze animals, or it could hold valuable produce, including bushes of wild fruits or other useful plant matter such as rushes and reeds, which were brought into the home to use as flooring. These smaller gathering tasks were, again, often relegated to women and children. The poorest in society in various regions tended to consume a mainly vegetarian diet, eating only low-quality meat from older animals that had outgrown their use as working beasts. Anything that a woman could bring to the house through extra work was important to the survival of the family unit.[5]

Among the most common kinds of tasks peasant women undertook were those related to textiles. All the wool gathered from sheep had to be processed before it was used, and for much of our period, this initial processing was done at a local level. Cloth may have been

refined, decorated, and turned into luxurious products in towns and urban centers, but it was initially purchased in a fairly raw form from rural areas. Women would shear sheep on their smallholdings and then, using their distaffs, spin wool—or linen or flax—into threads that would be sent to looms in their local town or village, where they would be processed.[6] The image of a woman with a distaff was pervasive in the medieval period, and countless images can be found of women, from peasants depicted in the margins of a manuscript to glorious multicolor full-scale images of the Virgin Mary, using distaffs.

That even the most holy woman in Christianity was associated with this task shows the importance of textile work to medieval Europeans. Around 1100, the bishop of Rennes in Brittany wrote a poem called the *Book of Ten Chapters*, and within his fourth chapter he praises women who use the spindle and weave yarn, proclaiming that, "if they were lacking, the quality of our life would decline." In the same vein, in the following century, Italian noble Philip of Novara explained that women of all classes should learn how to spin and sew, because then the poor would have a skill that could earn them money, and the rich would understand how others in society had to work. He too highlights that there is great reward and no shame to be found in these skills, for even "the glorious mother of God deigned to work cloth and to spin."[7]

In fact, images of the Virgin Mary undertaking the ordinary tasks

of medieval women found great popularity as the period developed, particularly for religious women. The Virgin Mary was the ultimate role model for nuns, and whatever the Mother of God did, so too should they. Both manuscripts and paintings increasingly depicted Mary at a loom or doing other daily household chores.[8]

As the medieval period progressed, towns and cities began to grow. Even the devastation of the Black Death in the mid-fourteenth century did not curtail the trend of people moving from the countryside to live together in these more developed areas. This fundamental change in how people lived had huge repercussions for peasant women, as they too were part of this movement. Over time, these migrants found that their lives as urban housewives diverged more and more from those of their rural counterparts. While many tasks were still common—the family still needed feeding and clothing, and even families in towns kept small livestock such as chickens that needed tending—a whole new world of work opened up. And, alongside it, as the centuries progressed, a new social status also developed: the professional woman.

URBAN WOMEN

In the Middle Ages, urban women had perhaps some of the most diverse life experiences, depending on where in Europe they lived. Although much of what is discussed in this book is, by its nature, generalized, many common threads can be pulled. But in terms of participation in the urban economy, there was a stark divide between women in southern Europe and those in the north and west during this time. Italian women in particular were far more restricted than women in England, France, the Low Countries, Germany, and the Iberian Peninsula.

Italian women endured far stronger cultural expectations in terms of what we might consider traditionally feminine roles. They were not to leave the parental home until marriage, and they usually married young, typically in their mid-teenage years. While women everywhere were expected to produce children for their husbands, Italian women tended to start younger because of their lower marriage age. The rest of Europe had an average marriage age of mid- to late twenties, which meant that Italian women were getting married around ten years earlier and thus tended to have several more children than their northern and western counterparts. A stronger cohesiveness of the extended family in this region

←← Peasants often appear in the decorations on calendar pages, as they were commonly engaged in seasonal work tasks. This image for February shows a snowy farmyard with some peasants at work in the cold while others sit inside warming their feet by a fire.

Limbourg brothers (active c. 1400–1416)
Très Riches Heures du Duc de Berry, fol. 2v, France, 1412–16
Musée Condé, Chantilly, France; MS 65/1284

↓ As well as depicting everyday tasks, some marginalia in medieval manuscripts was made solely to entertain. Here, a woman uses her distaff to joust with a knight.

Arthurian Romances (detail), fol. 329r, France, 1275–1300
Yale University Library, New Haven, CT; Beinecke MS 229

Women had very different legal rights across Europe. Some regions, such as the Iberian Peninsula, gave women more autonomy, as shown by this woman taking an oath before King James I of Aragon.

Capbreu de Clayra et de Millas (detail), Catalonia, 1292
Archives Départementales des Pyrénées-Orientales, Perpignan, France

meant there was less pressure on women to earn money to support the household. On top of this, Italian laws were more restrictive for women. In Italy and nearby areas, women were barred from entering a binding agreement without male approval, but other regions, such as Iberia, guaranteed women an equal inheritance share alongside their brothers and allowed them to enter contracts without male consent.[9]

Moreover, while today people tend to associate monarchy with repression and democracy with freedom, in terms of medieval women's participation in society, the situation was usually reversed. In countries and territories where rulership was inherited, be those monarchies, dukedoms, or any other form of noble rule, there were inevitably examples of female inheritance. Whether these regions welcomed female succession, or all the male heirs had died, women would eventually become queens, duchesses, countesses—leaders. Though there could still be resistance to these women in charge, as will be explored in chapter III, the regular appearance of women in leadership positions led to more acceptance of women's participation in other levels of society. In Italy and similar territories that were governed by republican regimes, participation in public life depended on lottery or election, and thus it was far easier to exclude women and have all-male offices. For these reasons, many of the professions open to medieval European women centered around the regions where they were granted more freedom and opportunity.

In urban regions, work opportunities were numerous and socially acceptable. From the eleventh century, women had become more and more visible working outside the home. Urban centers began to grow in the thirteenth century, and by around 1300, most towns and cities had attained the greatest populations they would see throughout the medieval period—the upcoming devastation of the Black Death would halt that growth. At this time, the largest

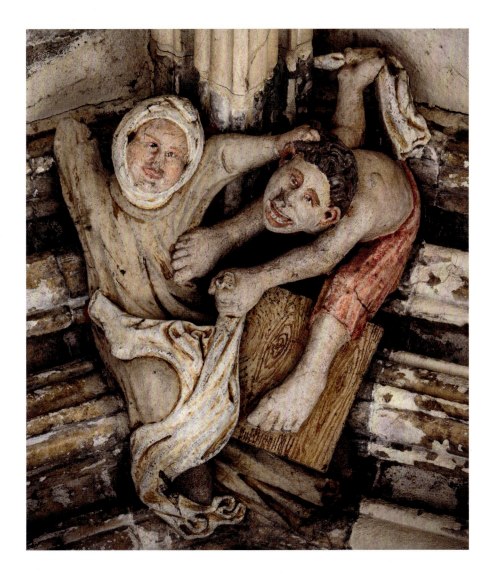

Many depictions of peasant women can be found in manuscripts, but peasants themselves would not have had access to books to see these images. They would, however, have access to artwork in churches, which provided a chance to see reflections of themselves in art that usually had a moral lesson. This stone ceiling carving, known as a roof boss, shows a peasant woman apprehending a thief who has tried to steal her washing.

Roof boss, early 14th century
Norwich Cathedral cloister, England

Workshops were family-run businesses, and women were expected to participate just as much as men. This manuscript miniature shows a man, woman, and child undertaking tasks in a workshop, the woman spinning with her distaff.

Jean Bourdichon (c. 1457–1521)
The Four Conditions of Society: Work, leaf, France, 15th century
Bibliothèque de l'Ecole des Beaux-Arts, Paris; Mn.Mas 92

city in Europe is thought to have been Paris, with an estimated two hundred thousand residents.[10] As the period progressed, women from the countryside moved to urban regions in the hopes of better opportunities and a better life.

Even if women's work was not always appreciated on the same level as men's, it was recognized and understood that women played a key role in keeping society running. Thus, men in these new urban centers could not survive on their own—they needed wives, and these wives could not be responsible for the home alone. Part of women's importance was indeed in keeping the household running by managing servants and children and feeding their husbands, but women took on a far more central role in the economy than we might expect.

Over the Middle Ages, a specific business model developed across northern and western Europe that revolved around the family unit. It was not always the case that women stayed home while the men went out to work. A man's work centered on his home or, more specifically, a connected workshop. While communal-work buildings existed in large industries, many trades and professions took place in individual shops and workshops, which sold their produce directly to the purchaser or to merchants. This meant a woman would be at the heart of the business, and she was expected to play an equal role even at times when she was not expected to do the physical labor of the profession. The male head may have been the craftsman who was making the product and training apprentices, but his wife and daughters were expected to provide food for them, clean the workshop, help organize the finances and manage the budget, and get involved in selling the product. In many instances, they were also expected to learn how to do the physical craft or at least parts of it.

Just as a noblewoman needed to know the details of her husband's estates so she could care for them while he was away, the wife of a craftsman was expected to know her husband's trade. Writer Christine de Pisan's 1405 work *The Treasure of the City of Ladies* explains that the wife "should learn all the shop details so that she can properly supervise the workers when her husband is away or not paying attention." In fact, the expectation that businesses would be run by a family unit is exemplified in regulations in some European cities that forbade a single man to establish a shop—he had to be married to do so.[11] The fundamental running of a business in most of medieval Europe, therefore, meant women found positions in a wide variety of sectors.

HOSPITALITY

As we have seen, many industries in which women flourished were those that were considered an extension of their role within the home. This meant that a variety of jobs classed as "hospitality" were populated by women. As towns and cities grew in size, fewer and fewer of their inhabitants were growing their own food, and there was a boom in shops and market stalls where people could purchase what they needed. Women dominated this sphere, and the rent lists

for the city of Bruges in Flanders demonstrate this clearly: in 1304, women held fifty of the fifty-five stalls in the cheese market, while the following year, eighty-three of the ninety-three fruit stalls set up during Lent belonged to women. This was not unique to Bruges, but a story seen time and again across Europe; in England, fifteen of the twenty poulterers listed in the 1290–91 roll of Wallingford were women, while the Nottingham poultry market had long been known as the "Womanmarket."[12]

As the period developed, there was a new arena for providing food and drink in the form of inns, taverns, and alehouses. Even though many people spent much of their life within a small radius of where they were born, there were plenty of opportunities for travel during the Middle Ages. Whether one was a merchant traveling the continent with one's wares, a knight or noble moving between his estates and court, or a pilgrim on a holy journey to shrines, churches, and religious sites, a person could have many reasons to find themselves on the road passing through an unknown town. Even within one's own town or city, people needed a place to socialize. Inns, taverns, and alehouses grew through the period to cater to these needs.

Whereas we may think of these terms as generally interchangeable, there was actually a distinction to these establishments in the medieval period: inns provided accommodation and full hot meals; alehouses, as the name suggests, sold ale; and taverns tended to have a higher caliber of drink, as they sold wine, and usually had a small offering of food. These boundaries were not always adhered to, and most importantly, these places were not restricted to serving only travelers. Locals would spend much of their time in these establishments—they were a communal area where gossip was spread,

business was conducted, physicians were hired, and marriage announcements were made. As alehouses were often disdained as places of drunken debauchery, more respectable people could be found at inns or taverns.[13]

Taverns, inns, and alehouses were liminal spaces, where the high and mighty could mix with the local rabble, where foreigners could find a bite to eat and a place to rest their head, and where respectable business deals could be made while rubbing shoulders with the unsavory parts of society. With alcohol at the heart of the establishment, though, these places could balance on a knife's edge of respectability. Drunkenness was not tolerated in the medieval period, and places that encouraged such depravity were looked down upon. The women who worked in these establishments could risk their reputation. Even though some families ran respectable, successful inns, wives and daughters serving in these buildings were sometimes regarded with suspicion—and this was not always without reason.

Prostitution is often referred to as the world's oldest profession, and it certainly proliferated at different times and places across medieval Europe. Inns, alehouses, and taverns were places where prostitution was commonly found. There were many cases of a male owner selling the services of his wife, daughters, or sisters from his premises—and some cases of women encouraging this too.[14] It was therefore not completely without reason that women working in these places could find themselves pegged with an unsavory reputation.

For many women involved in prostitution, it was not a long-term career. There was little lasting demand for their trade in the small villages and towns, particularly at the start of the period, as travelers could be few and far between, and the local men expressed less of a need for these services. It was more common that women were forced into temporary prostitution during times of hardship as a way to supplement their income, and this was usually an informal arrangement between prostitute and client in one of their homes, or they might find a room in a tavern; it was not always necessary

Inns, alehouses, and taverns could gain unsavory reputations for accommodating drunken debauchery, which was looked down upon in medieval society. The women who worked in such places could find their own reputations tarnished as a result. This scene shows some of the sinful behaviors associated with these establishments, including prostitution and drunkenness.

Valerius Maximus, *Memorable Deeds and Sayings*, fol. 51r, France, 15th century
Bibliothèque Nationale de France, Paris; Français 6185

for a woman to offer this service at a brothel. Across Europe, migrants sometimes had fewer choices of work or less protection under local laws, and so they were more vulnerable to employment as prostitutes than other peasant women. A 1395 survey in Bologna, Italy, shows that the profession most assigned to women was that of prostitute, and the majority so assigned were foreign women.[15]

Since any woman could temporarily turn to prostitution during difficult times, as the Middle Ages progressed and towns and cities increased in size and number, prostitution also grew. Various towns in the Low Countries became renowned for prostitution because they were such hubs of international trade. Merchants from all over Europe would travel to towns like Bruges for months at a time for business, and these were either young, single men or married men who had not brought their families with them. Both scenarios led to a demand for sexual services. But when the economy dipped or war broke out, these urban centers emptied of their merchants, and the demand for sex dropped.[16]

In times of higher demand, there was a greater variety of places where one could procure such services. Brothels took several forms, but generally prostitutes could be found in three locations: what we

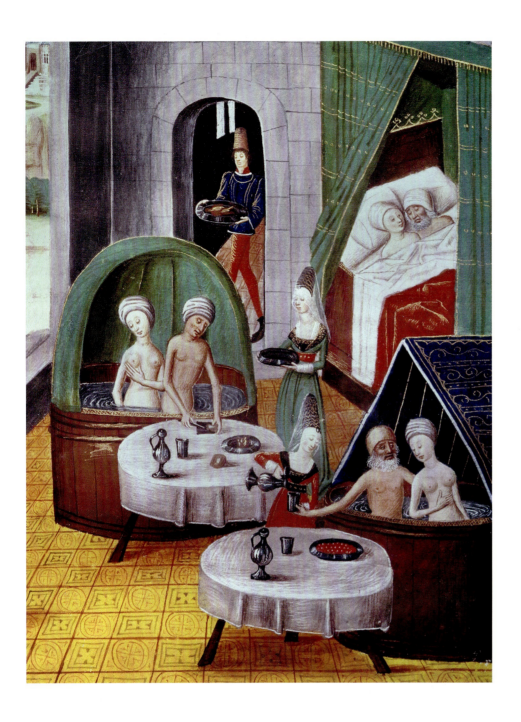

might think of as a brothel, a house with numerous rooms where multiple women worked; single rooms with a hearth and sleeping area found scattered across a town; and bathhouses. Like inns and taverns, bathhouses were not solely used for prostitution. In a time when only the most elite had bathrooms in their manor houses, most people in at least semi-urban areas wished to visit a bathhouse to have a proper cleaning. Bathhouses were social hubs on a par with inns, where people could meet to agree on business or share gossip over a meal. But any gathering place with semiprivate areas can lead to temptation, and it was not unusual to find prostitutes operating out of bathhouses. This was particularly popular earlier in our period, but as the Middle Ages drew to a close, it became far more common to solicit a prostitute from a specialist house.[17]

European authorities were indecisive about how to deal with

Bathhouses were communal areas where medieval Europeans could gather to wash and socialize, but they could also be fronts for prostitution. Though prostitution in bathhouses had fallen out of fashion by the time this image was made, it shows how men could meet with these women and then take them to private areas. This image was intended as a criticism of greed and sin, a warning to the manuscript's reader.

Valerius Maximus, *Memorable Deeds and Sayings* (detail), fol. 372r, 15th century Bibliotheque de L'Arsenal, France (Paris); Ms-5196 reserve

prostitution, and each in turn tried a variety of policies. In Christian nations, sex outside of marriage was forbidden, and authorities did not want to encourage sin. Various places tried outright bans on prostitution, but the repeated legislation against it shows that they were unsuccessful. In many locations where full bans were implemented, a certain level of practice was tacitly accepted by simply fining brothel keepers. This in effect acted as a licensing fee, as records show repeat offenders turning up time and again, without any real evidence that authorities were truly attempting to stamp out the trade.[18]

Some level of begrudging acceptance eventually spread across towns, cities, and territories. While society perceived prostitution as sinful, authorities also recognized that demand needed to be met and that if they could regulate the practice, they could help maintain wider law and order. The irony was also not lost on many that in plenty of regions the highest demand for prostitutes came from men of the church. The next step was to allow limited brothels but confine the prostitutes to particular areas in the city to protect the wider population. These streets picked up names related to the trade that still survive to this day; one somewhat more polite example is the numerous thoroughfares called "Grope Lane," a name often later changed to "Grape Lane" to make it more acceptable.[19]

Besides restricting prostitutes to particular areas of town, further limitations were placed upon them both to mark them as lesser than other "proper" women in society and to reduce risk of social disorder. In London, prostitutes were required to wear hoods of multicolor cloth; parts of France introduced particular sleeves and headdresses; and Italy forced them to wear a strip of yellow cloth. Other regions banned prostitutes from wearing respectable headdresses or ordered them to wear particular jewelry.[20] With prostitutes suitably highlighted to the world around them and confined to particular streets or buildings, authorities could now benefit from the profits of prostitution with a clearer conscience. As the Middle Ages drew to an end, countless regions in Europe had officially run brothels.

Although rules against prostitutes could be harsh, including banning them from entering the city between certain hours of the day and banishing them altogether during the (many) religious holidays, there was a recognition that women could be coerced into selling sex. The rules that officials drew up were in part intended to prevent this, and while some places did little to help women, many regions introduced a variety of laws to prevent them from being forced into the trade, such as making it illegal for people to hold debts over prostitutes and make them work to pay off their debt. Furthermore, multiple religious institutions set up homes to house and try to reform prostitutes, though these places frequently lacked sufficient support to continue. Unfortunately, many peasant women who came to the city to make a better life for themselves ended up being exploited.

Though some women became prostitutes, numerous rural women traveled to towns and cities with the intention to serve in a home. Having a servant was not limited to the wealthy. In fact, during

←← Though there were strict religious rules about sex outside of marriage, medieval romances were filled with couples bending these dictates. These images illustrate the story of Troilus and Criseyde spending the night together, as told by Italian writer Giovanni Boccaccio in his poem about the couple.

Giovanni Boccaccio, *Il Filostrato*, fol. 26r, France, 15th century Bodleian Libraries, University of Oxford, England; MS. Douce 331

↓ Art in public places often had lessons to teach. Not all women who were so depicted were there to be emulated; some were to serve as warnings—as in this church wall painting depicting the biblical Salome (*foreground*), who was partially responsible for the murder of Saint John the Baptist.

Martyrdom of Saint John the Baptist, fresco (detail), c. 1470 Saint Peter and Saint Paul's Church, Pickering, England

the Middle Ages, most households—apart from the very poorest—employed domestic help. Less wealthy rural families may have had only one servant, but those living in towns tended to have several servants in their homes, and the great noble families could have a large number of servants. Being a servant was not a specifically feminine occupation, and in fact, male servants were preferred in many areas. Male servants were preferred in regions with plenty of arable farmland, whereas female servants were more common in towns and cities. Male servants undertook physical labor such as fetching and carrying items, stewarding the house, caring for horses, cooking and serving food, and helping work the land. Female servants undertook tasks suitable to their gender, usually an extension of the roles of a wife. They would care for the women and children of the house, cook, clean, manage other servants, and tend to any livestock.[21] If a household could afford only one servant, it was more likely to employ a woman to undertake the multiple tasks expected, but households that could afford many servants tended to have mostly men and just a couple of women.[22]

In northern and western Europe, where women married later, it was common for families to send their teenage daughters to work. This not only amassed income for the household, or for the girl herself to save for her marriage, but also was intended to teach her the skills that she would need to run her own household once she was married. This service was expected for women of all statuses, though noble girls went to serve in households of other nobles in a much gentler and more respectable way than poorer girls, who would experience the hard labor of being a servant. Girls were sent to work from the age of twelve onward—when they were canonically of age according to the church—and if there was not a work position within their own household then they would travel elsewhere.

The 1379 poll tax for Howden and Howdenshire in England demonstrates the popularity of this profession, as just shy of 70 percent of daughters over the age of sixteen still living at home were listed as servants. While this practice was very common in countries like England and France, southern Europeans were appalled when they heard about it. Around 1500, a Venetian diplomat to England reported back home in shock that English children of all levels of society were sent into service.[23] In his society, to do so was akin to sending one's daughter into prostitution. This was in sharp contrast to English culture, which viewed the experience as honorable and even necessary for all women, including the nobility.

CRAFTS AND TRADES

Outside of hospitality, working in a skilled trade was the next most common profession for women during the Middle Ages. As women were considered central to the family-unit model of running a business, it was inevitable that they would be hands-on with the physicality of the profession, learning it for themselves. Christine de Pisan was not alone in expecting women to step in when their male relatives needed assistance. As the period progressed and professionalization of trades increased, there became a stronger shared vision of protecting the secrets of a trade and keeping it within the family. Sons would train in the same profession as their father, uncles, and brothers, and guild membership became hereditary. Women were included in this family circle—daughters married apprentices or family friends who were in the same trade, and widows were often expected to keep their husband's shop running after his death. If a man had only daughters, then he might expect to pass his business to one of them, and her husband, by extension, was expected to pick up the same trade. Women, therefore, needed to know important details about the craft and running a business in order to continue the line of inheritance.

Many historians have undertaken studies of sources to determine the level of participation of medieval women in the European workforce, but finding women within these scant documents can be tricky. The standard sources used to identify male workers by their nature excluded women. Tax documents tended to focus only on the occupation of the head of household and ignore other members of the family unit who were also earning a living, thus excluding women unless they were widows who headed their own household. Other documents, such as payment lists for workers, can provide very little detail as they may not name workers or mention their gender. In later periods, guild records can be used to identify male tradesmen, but the majority of European trade guilds excluded

In this illustration, a woman cooks sweet bread over a fire. Unless a family had servants, it was usually the woman's duty to cook meals for her family. Women could also work in hospitality by providing food for others.

Pedanius Dioscorides, *Tractatus de herbis*, fol. 142r, France (Bourg), 1458 Biblioteca Estense, Modena, Italy; alpha.l.09.28

The margins of manuscripts are filled with images of women in daily life—the lower right edge of this page has a woman holding a spoon and a bread trough.

Book of hours (detail), fol. 118r, northeastern France or western Flanders, 1275–1300 Walters Art Museum, Baltimore; W.39

women or severely limited their participation. Women were also far likelier than men to undertake temporary and seasonal work, changing professions multiple times through their lives, making it harder to trace them across already scarce records. What remain are very unsatisfactory statistics and case studies that cannot ever fully represent the true inclusion of women in the medieval workforce.

Some patterns, however, do emerge from these crucial studies. In general, women across Europe were paid significantly less than their male counterparts for the same work; women frequently received half to two-thirds of the wages of men. This was partially due to an expectation that women could not fulfill a role to the same level as a man, but it also took inspiration from the Bible, as Leviticus recommended a payment ratio of three to five for women to men.[24] This meant that sometimes women's labor was in great demand, as it was a cheap method of outsourcing during times of economic difficulty or on large projects that required many workers. There were certain industries in which women dominated—around 50 percent of linen merchants and 90 percent of silk weavers identified in Paris at the turn of the fourteenth century were women.[25] Moreover, women continued to be a strong minority across many professions, often representing 10–20 percent of workers in different trades.

When there is a dearth of written records, the art can illuminate these hidden women. Scenes of professions are abundant in manuscript art, with backdrops of workshops and working craftspeople at the center of many pages. Women are depicted in these scenes time and again, either performing the work themselves or undertaking some of the smaller tasks in the background. Even for professions where we can find almost no written records of women participating, women are shown doing so in art. How much the art represents the reality of the women whose records we cannot otherwise find, or whether they are more figurative than literal depictions—take, for example, the noblewomen and queens shown physically building Christine de Pisan's "City of Ladies" in various manuscripts—is up for debate, but the value of these images in helping us fill gaps in written records should not be ignored.

As we have seen that women were likelier to find work in professions that were deemed suitably feminine, it is not surprising that they were consistently most highly represented in the textile industry. For centuries, rural women had sheared their own sheep, harvested their own materials, and then processed threads and yarns at home to turn into textiles. As the Middle Ages progressed and textiles increasingly became more of an organized industry, it was natural for women to continue playing this central role. While rural women processed materials at a local level before sending the fruits of their labor into towns and cities to be fully processed into decorative cloth, the women who flocked to these towns and cities participated in all levels of the manufacturing chain.

Raw materials would be sent to urban centers, where women would wash and comb the wool and cloth, spin it into threads, weave it into materials, dye it, and produce clothing, tapestries, and other textile goods at looms—before any involvement in selling the finished

products.[26] In the first half of our period, women's skills in the industry were highly respected and unquestioned. Though men joined the profession, they were happy to be trained by women. Although it was less common for women to participate in the sale of the finished product than in making it, there are numerous examples of highly successful women who made a name for themselves in the trade.

Ysabel de Tremblay was a member of the upper bourgeoisie in Paris in the early fourteenth century. Her immediate family had connections in the city's government—her uncle and son served as aldermen—and her husband was a highly successful draper who supplied fine woolen cloth to the Count of Artois. When her husband died, Ysabel continued his business and found unrivaled success. For at least six months she held a virtual monopoly in providing luxury woolens to the French royal household; her cloth was used to make garments for all members of the royal family and was given by the monarchy as gifts to around 120 people. In 1316, she made over 2,200 *livres parisis* from sales to the royal household, a highly significant amount of money at the time. Ysabel's success was proven by that time, since three years prior she was recorded in the city's tax assessment as paying an astounding 75 *livres tournois* in taxes—this placed her among the top sixteen taxpayers and in the top 0.27 percent of all people in the city assessed that year.[27]

Women builders were represented allegorically in medieval depictions of Christine de Pisan's *The Book of the City of Ladies*. In this manuscript miniature, on the left, Christine meets with the personifications of Reason, Rectitude, and Justice, who encourage her to construct a city for famous women. At the right, Christine is shown following their advice.

Master of the Cité des Dames (active 1400–1415)
Christine de Pisan, *The Book of the City of Ladies*, fol. 2r, France (Paris), 1400–1410
Bibliothèque Nationale de France, Paris; Français 607

Women congregated in towns and cities to produce textiles, as the industry was significant enough that it needed more space than a home could provide. Certain areas of Europe dominated the cloth trade, particularly England, with its highly sought wool, and the Low Countries, which were renowned for their processing of cloth. From the start of the Middle Ages to around the early thirteenth century, many women gathered in buildings known as gynaeceums to process cloth. Women could enter these workshops even as young girls to learn how to produce materials, and though they were usually provided with meals, conditions could be dismal. Gynaeceums were often filled with slaves or criminals, and prostitutes were known to work out of them, tarnishing the reputation of all the shop's women employees.[28] These institutions eventually disappeared, and other types of processing centers took their place. As communities of beguines—religious laywomen who we will return to in the next chapter—began to emerge in the middle of the thirteenth century, they started to take over much of the lower level of production. Due to their dedication to Christianity and a chaste life, they escaped some of the bad reputation that their predecessors had experienced, but they tended to be given the least skilled jobs of washing the cloth and basic processing.[29]

When the thirteenth century arrived, however, women began to find their hegemony of the textile profession challenged by men. Europe was beginning to shift toward professionalization of work across many different trades and, as in the numerous industries we will discuss, it became more important for an individual to become highly skilled in one profession. Developments in technology, the increase in towns and cities where knowledge could be shared and advanced, and the emergence of a bourgeois, mercantile class leading to an increase in trade and its profitability all led to men taking a greater share of the workforce. Therefore, they restricted entry into their trades by creating guilds that looked after their own.

Guilds were formed to protect those who engaged in a trade or profession in cities or large towns. They created strict rules: they limited who could work in the city to those who were guild members, regulated prices and wages, managed trade practices, judged

pie finit fciue ff. denda
ne feñtes quid kipit. s.c. uencus
ne dit̃
n̈ fuí

the quality of a craftsperson's work, and helped facilitate the training of apprentices. Guild membership could be extended to women, but their access was often limited in scope. Most of the time, women could join only if they were related to a male guild member. Moreover, many of the trades that women dominated were not considered skilled enough to require guilds.

There were some female-dominated guilds across Europe, notably in Paris, Rouen, and Cologne, but these were few and far between. Even if women were admitted as members, they were rarely full members with the right to vote in guild matters or to wear the guild livery.[30] As such, most guilds were looking out for the interests of men in their profession, and any care for women came as an afterthought when the male members wished to extend protection or luxuries to their female relatives. By the end of the fifteenth century, it was difficult for anyone to undertake a skilled trade without being a member of a guild, and so most women had been pushed back into the domestic sphere.

This was certainly the case in the textile industry. As the fourteenth and fifteenth centuries arrived, men assumed a larger role in the industry. In Bruges, 25 percent of the male population was engaged in the cloth trade, while in Leiden—also at the heart of the industry—half of adult males were employed in drapery.[31] Though women continued to work at less-skilled jobs, as the beguines did, an increasing number of men began to take the more skilled—and thus better paid and more highly respected—roles, such as fabric dyer. As Leiden increased its cloth production, large numbers of migrants moved into the town to take advantage of the flourishing industry. By the time the medieval period drew to a close, male

domination of the trade in the city was complete: out of around two thousand adults working in the industry, only about one hundred were women.[32]

The roots of this change in gender balance went back to at least the thirteenth century, when John of Garland, a teacher in Paris, wrote a dictionary of Latin terms for everyday activities. In his writing, he noted that "certain men are usurping for themselves the offices of women."[33] Brewing was another stark example of this. Whereas the start of the period saw most brewing taking place in small-scale domestic spheres, technology and professionalization once again spelled the end of female dominance. Ale, with its short shelf life, began to be replaced by beer brewed from hops. Beer kept for much longer than ale, meaning production became more commercialized as it could be mass produced and stored.[34] Now that production was moving outside the home and into the realms of moneymaking, men started to take over brewing themselves.

Despite this gradual shift across the later Middle Ages, for most of our period, wives still worked alongside their husbands at their trade, and there was a general expectation that a widow might wish to continue her husband's work after his death to support herself and their children. This was for the benefit not just of the woman but also for those who had been working for her husband, as his death could lead to their unemployment. Men were not embarrassed to be trained by a woman, and they were willing to follow legal routes to enforce the cultural expectation placed upon a widow. In one instance, in 1429, Beatrix Goscelyn, the wife of a London ironmonger, was sued by her husband's apprentice when she sold her husband's business after his death. The apprentice argued that "by the law and custom of the city and will of the deceased [she] ought to have kept up his household and instructed his apprentices."[35] Training as an apprentice was a long service, generally anticipated to take around seven years, and so it is easy to understand why this apprentice did not wish to lose the time he had invested or try to find another instructor.

Although women were frequently involved in the same trade as their husbands, there are plenty of examples of medieval professional women working in different industries. Women in northern and western Europe had a significant degree of freedom to undertake work that suited them or that would bring money to the household, and they could do so without strict supervision by their husbands. A seamstress was trusted to go to work while her husband sold wine, and a goldsmith had no problem with his wife working as a spice merchant. But many couples found success when they worked together, and their enterprise could involve other family members

←← Even trades we think of as masculine had women in assistant roles. In the back of a woodworking shop in this image, a woman can be seen working bellows.

Balthasar Behem Codex (detail), fol. 284r, Poland, c. 1506 Biblioteka Jagiellońska, Kraków, Poland; BJ Rkp. 16 IV

↓ Though we cannot always name specific women working in trades, tradeswomen constantly show up in artwork. This scene from the life of Saint Eligius, a seventh-century goldsmith and bishop, shows his workshop, where among his assistants is a woman *(far right)* hammering a product into shape.

Master of Balaam (active 15th century) *Saint Eligius in His Workshop* (detail), Germany, 1440–60 Engraving on paper, 4½ × 7¾ in. (11.5 × 18.5 cm) Rijksmuseum, Amsterdam

too. Around 1440, soap maker Andreu Dea Brull formed a company with a merchant named Bartholomeu Sagarra and his mother, Eulalia, in Barcelona. The Sagarras were the financial backers of the business, with Bartholomeu investing 30 florins and his mother a far more significant 200 florins. Using their money, they purchased the raw materials for Andreu to create the soaps. The Sagarras then used their connections as merchants to sell the soaps and manage the accounts.[36] Eulalia was clearly important in this partnership for her financial contribution, and it is likely that she also would have been involved in other aspects of the business and valued for her abilities and intelligence.

Women were also found in particularly specialist crafts. Glaziers grew in demand as the medieval period progressed, and as the wealthy became wealthier and began to commission larger and grander projects, glaziers' services were ever more important. Stained glass windows in particular were ubiquitous, casting colored light in churches and palaces alike. Initially, glaziers saw their products through from start to finish, blowing their own glass and then shaping, decorating, and fitting it. This alienated women, as glassblowing was difficult, physical labor seen as unsuitable for their sex. But in the 1280s, the industry changed rapidly. From then until 1300, glass technologies and skills developed, resulting in products that were thinner and clearer and that could be made as large single pieces. At this point, glaziers diverged between those who physically made the glass and those who decorated it, the latter role providing opportunities for women.

Glazing was a surprisingly accessible trade for those prepared to learn the skills. Evidence suggests that many glaziers may have been illiterate, as there are plenty of examples of mistakes in written inscriptions in windows. Earlier in the medieval period, work was not particularly abundant for glaziers, meaning they were often itinerant, traveling from town to town or between a noble's estates to find new projects. A traveling lifestyle was seen as unsuitable for women, for it was associated with prostitution and other unseemliness, but the developments of the late thirteenth century helped to make glass more accessible and thus boosted the profession. More permanent glassworks with their own furnaces were established throughout Europe, such as one created in Paris on the eponymous rue de la Verrerie around 1185, and this helped center glaziers in big cities. The clients could now come to them to purchase their goods, rather than the other way around.

The Paris tax rolls from the turn of the fourteenth century once again reveal the place of women in the world of work, as numerous female glaziers are listed within. While most of them earned very little from their craft, one woman in particular, "Jehanne la verriere," was more successful, and this was perhaps attributable to her decision to run a shop for her wares. The shop can be traced in the tax records between 1296 and 1313 and might have existed longer than this; it also appears that Jehanne sold apothecary utensils that would have been made from glass. She is listed as living at the glassworks, alongside a few other glaziers, and this would have meant

she had easy access to the furnace there—likely the only place in Paris where one could make one's own glass—and this leads to the possibility that Jehanne actually made her own products. Her goods certainly proved popular, for in 1296 she is recorded as earning twenty-four sous. In contrast, the three female *verriers* listed in the 1292 tax roll earned only two sous each.[37]

Perhaps for our modern perception of gender roles in the medieval period, the most surprising place women could find work in Europe was on a construction site. Even today, many aspects of the construction industry remain male-dominated, but medieval women could find their place in the building industry. It is more difficult to trace individual women who took up construction, compared to other professions, because records are so scant and names are very rarely recorded in payments—but payments for women do notably occur with some frequency. Finding women working in construction is equally difficult in period artwork, and while there are a handful of examples of women shown truly helping on a worksite, it is more common for women to be portrayed as metaphorically building rather than actually doing so. Though war or disease, which produced a shortage of male laborers, could be catalysts for increasing women's participation in the building industry, their appearance was by no means limited to these circumstances.

In the late thirteenth century, developments in glazing techniques increased the skill required to make and decorate pieces of glass. As glass painting became a separate profession, more women were able to create beautiful pieces of stained glass. The makers of these pieces are unknown, but some women would have made similar artworks.

↖ *Head of a Woman*, France (Rouen), 14th century
Pot metal, white glass, vitreous paint, silver stain, 13 × 12⅝ in. (33 × 32 cm)
Metropolitan Museum of Art, Cloisters, New York

↑ *Stained Glass Panel with Female Donor* (detail), France, c. 1480
Pot metal, white glass, silver stain, 61½ × 17⅛ in. (156.2 × 43.5 cm)
Cleveland Museum of Art

Although we know that peasant women were employed in the construction industry, there are few artistic representations of them doing such work. Far more common are idealized images of noblewomen building, as in this example, where Countess Bertha of Paris builds a church in Vézelay, France, with the help of her maid.

Roman de Girart de Roussillon (detail), fol. 167v, Burgundy, 1448 Österreichische Nationalbibliothek, Vienna; Cod. 2549

The thirteenth century sparked an increase in opportunities for women in many parts of society, and this was certainly the case for female laborers, as instances of women being paid for construction work begin to occur.[38] The growth of towns and cities and their accompanying trades led to population surges and hence a need for new buildings in these areas. The people moving into the towns needed places to live, work, and pray, and builders were increasingly in demand. Women's physical limitations, alongside the extremely arduous manual labor that medieval building demanded, meant that they usually undertook the lowest-paying jobs on construction sites. The lowly, difficult tasks they performed, and the way society viewed women who participated in such a trade, meant that only the poorest of women tended to take on this kind of work.

Female laborers were most often tasked with transportation jobs, which included carrying water or building materials such as sand, stones, or mortar to the laborers who needed them. They helped to build and repair not only buildings but also roads, bridges, walls, and dams. Spain was an early adopter of female construction labor, and records list many cases of women engaging in manual labor throughout the later Middle Ages. Women were hired not only for small projects; in fifteenth-century Toledo, a handful of women were hired to assist with the construction of the city's cathedral, sweeping its floors, gathering lime, and working on the roof. France was not far behind its neighbor, and during the construction of Périgord College in Toulouse from 1365 to 1371, almost half of the workers were female. Women could also have a more distant connection to the building site through providing materials, as Englishwoman Katherine Lightfoot did in 1383, when she supplied two thousand painted tiles to Richard II for his bath in Sheen Palace.[39]

MEDICINE

As wives and mothers, women in medieval Europe were expected to have a level of medical knowledge in order to properly care for their families. Though professional doctors and local village healers existed, this was not a time of state-sponsored health care, and people needed to know how to treat everyday ailments. The Goodman of Paris, an unidentified Frenchman from the bourgeoisie, wrote an instruction manual for his much younger wife around 1393. The book contains all manner of useful advice that a woman of her status was expected to know, from how to be suitably pious and how to love and obey one's husband to how to instruct servants and manage a household. The plethora of recipes within included several for medicinal drinks and meals.[40]

While women may have consulted physicians and bought potions from merchants, they shared a network of knowledge both orally and through written recipes. Peasants to queens would share this information with one another; in 1374, Martha of Armagnac was suffering with breast pain after giving birth to her first child. Martha was Duchess of Girona and Countess of Cervera, having married the heir to the throne of Aragon, and though she may have consulted a doctor about her problem, she also wrote to her mother-in-law, Eleanor of Sicily, queen of Aragon, for help. Martha sent one of her husband's officers to the queen asking that she give him a recipe to treat the malady so that Martha could keep it for any future need.[41]

In the Aragonese court, royal women's knowledge of health care was not unusual, for in this same century a "master Joan" composed the *Tròtula*, a text on women's health, and dedicated it to a woman in the Aragon royal family.[42] While these women were at the pinnacle of society, it was expected that their peasant and professional sisters would maintain a level of medicinal knowledge as well. Those who were educated enough to read could purchase similar manuals that provided recipes to cure various illnesses, and those who were illiterate could pass on information orally.

Some women, though, were able to study medicine far more formally. The foremost medical school in Europe was founded in Salerno, Italy, in the ninth or tenth century, but the school's golden age began in 1077 when Constantine the African arrived. Shocked by the state of medical knowledge in Italy, Constantine was determined to share the knowledge gained from his travels across Africa, Asia, and the Middle East. Salerno soon became renowned for its healing knowledge, and a succession of skilled doctors at this medical school produced manuscripts about diseases and how to cure them. Even from its early days, it is clear that Salerno admitted women, and its doctors did not shy away from using the medical knowledge of women, trained or not; in their manuscripts, the male

A woman helps a man finish building a church in this woodcut illustration. Records from various European countries show the presence of women on the building sites of churches and cathedrals.

Master of the Amsterdam Cabinet (c. 1470–1500) (attributed)
The Mirror of the Human Receptacle with the Gospels and Epistles . . . , image 239 (Speyer, Germany: Peter Drach), c. 1495
Library of Congress, Washington, DC; Incun. X .S725

authors occasionally cite the "women of Salerno" as the source of information on cures. This reputation spread across Europe—in a twelfth-century story composed by Marie of France, the aunt of the story's princess studied medicine at Salerno for thirty years.[43] Marie's readers were expected to recognize Salerno as a reputable institution and therefore understand that the character was highly knowledgeable in medicine.

That there was a period when it was considered acceptable for women to study medicine is exemplified by an unrealized plan by a French lawyer and official, Pierre Dubois, in 1309. Christian Europe had been entangled in conflicts and crusades in the Holy Land for centuries, and Pierre had an idea, which he brought to the French king, to try to convert the region once and for all. Pierre envisioned a series of schools that would train noble boys and girls. The most beautiful and intelligent girls would, when they came of age, be sent to the Holy Land and even into Asia to marry into noble and rich families of nonbelievers. They would then convert those around them through the admiration that they would inspire with their skills. In order to fulfill this task, the girls would be educated in a number of languages, theology and logic, and medicine and surgery. Pierre expected that this medical training, in particular, would make the girls highly desirable, not only for its benefit to their households when they married but because it could also help them treat local women, who would thus become easier to convert.[44] Though the plans never came to fruition, that the official medical instruction of

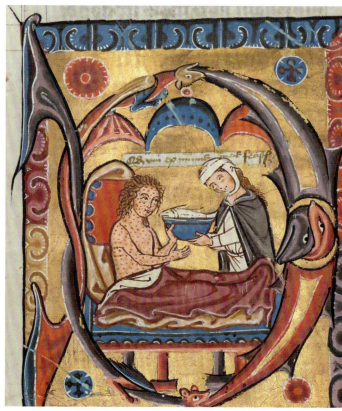

women was deemed central to a European- and Christian-wide plan to convert the wider world speaks volumes.

When we actually trace women who practiced medicine formally, though, the story becomes a lot murkier. Surviving official records naming female medics are few and far between, even though it is clear that women were practicing medicine at a variety of levels. Much of our evidence of female doctors comes from the fourteenth century onward when, as in other professions, a crackdown was happening across Europe to restrict women's participation. Though women were still expected to have some medical influence in their homes, the last two centuries of the Middle Ages saw an aggressive persecution of women practicing medicine. Just as male-dominated guilds pushed women to the fringes of crafts and trades, so too did the increasing professionalization of medicine turn against women.

Despite Pierre's proposals, France was one of the early adopters of the marginalization of women physicians. From the late thirteenth century, the medical faculty of the university at Paris advocated for a suppression of untrained medical practitioners—both male and female. They wanted to ensure that only those who were licensed could shoulder the significant responsibility of caring for the health of the nation, and that meant those who had studied with them and were therefore under their control. In 1322, just over a decade after Pierre's ambitious plans, a series of trials was held in Paris against unlicensed healers. One of the accused was Jacoba Felicie, who had been practicing medicine on men and women. The prosecution argued that if women were not allowed to practice law in the city, then they certainly should not be allowed to partake in something as important as health care, where they could kill somebody.[45]

Other countries followed France's lead. In 1329, the Kingdom of Valencia in Spain passed a law that specifically barred women from practicing medicine or providing potions, though they were allowed to care for small children and other women without the use of potions. Some countries were slower in their official denunciation of women—for example, the first petition found in England requesting the ban of women from practicing medicine was not until a century later, in 1421—but by the end of the Middle Ages, a significant portion of Europe expected the practice of medicine to be the preserve of men, even if this did not always follow in reality.[46]

One way that medieval women could cling to performing medicine professionally, apart from being a nun in a convent hospital, was through treating other women. There is ample evidence that early female physicians, surgeons, and apothecaries cared for both men and women and that female medical practitioners were not always expected to treat only women. But as the Middle Ages drew to a close, and women found themselves shut out of the profession, the excuse of female modesty was a way for them to continue their trade.

While medieval women could be examined by male doctors, certain aspects of their health care, such as childbirth and gynecological problems, were considered more suitably handled by other women. Men certainly did have an interest in gynecology, and they both wrote and read manuscripts that dealt with the subject. But regardless

→ Women were expected to know various treatments for illnesses so that they could care for their family members and others in their community. In this picture, a woman reads from a recipe book as she makes medicine over a fire.

The Blinding of Tobit, *Bible Historiale of Edward IV* (detail), fol. 18r, southern Netherlands (Bruges), c. 1479 British Library, London; Royal 15 D. I

↘↘ Women's knowledge of medicine could lead to suspicion—this stained glass window shows a woman carrying poison to use against Saint Germain of Paris. Men often raised the prospect that a woman practicing medicine could kill someone as an argument to ban them from the profession.

Woman Dispensing Poison from the Legend of Saint Germain of Paris (detail), France, 1245–47 Stained glass panel, 25⅛ × 15¾ in. (63.8 × 40 cm) Metropolitan Museum of Art, Cloisters, New York

of their knowledge about afflictions and potential cures, medieval modesty meant that it was considered improper for a man to inspect a woman's genitals. Male doctors, then, would always require female assistants to perform gynecological examinations, meaning women could never be completely removed from the medical practice.

Throughout the Middle Ages, women were commonly employed as midwives. Childbirth was a strictly female affair. In the upper echelons of the nobility, women would retreat into confinement for about a month before a baby was due, into all-female chambers surrounding the mother-to-be. Though a prolonged confinement was less practical for peasant women, even they were expected to have only female attendants when the time came to give birth. Translations of the word "midwife" from various European languages, combined with descriptions of the term in works like the thirteenth-century encyclopedia of Bartholomew the Englishman, all make it clear that to the medieval mind, a midwife was only ever a woman.[47]

Christian women certainly performed medical care in a plethora of guises through the Middle Ages, yet it appears that in Europe, there may have been a preference for this work to be undertaken instead by Jewish or Muslim women. Various studies of known female doctors across Europe consistently show a high proportion of women of these religions in practice.[48] Whereas Christian women were expected to undertake medical care in the home through producing, buying, and administering potions and otherwise feeding and caring for the sick, sensibilities may have led to a preference for "proper" women not to do so professionally; minority practitioners were therefore accepted as a way to provide women's health care without having to worry about any social consequences.

On the periphery of health care across medieval society was the need to employ wet nurses. In a time before formulated milk, there was always a need for women to step in to feed newborns, including abandoned children and those whose mother had died in childbirth.

Moreover, there was a growing trend among noblewomen of not breastfeeding. At lower levels of the social order, wet nurses could be employed through a local hospital, but at the upper echelons, wet nurse was a privileged profession.

For those poorer children in society, a wet nurse was assigned from whomever was available, either a peasant or a professional woman. The Hôpital du Saint-Esprit in Marseille, founded in 1188, regularly had infants in its care and created a system for hiring wet nurses that would have been familiar to other European institutions. The hospital had a room where the babies could sleep, and at times it hired a resident wet nurse, but generally it tried to place infants within the homes of wet nurses in the town's community; the nurses were expected to care for the child until it was weaned. For a significant period, wages for this work remained low, but upon the devastation of the population by the Black Death, demand naturally exploded, and so did wages. At the start of the fourteenth century, monthly wages for wet nurses slowly rose from one sous to four or five sous, but as plague hit in 1348, wages shot up to over twenty-six sous a month, and by the start of the following century, they hit a high of sixty-four sous a month.[49]

The employment of women who became wet nurses was dictated by demand and whether they were lactating. And there is plenty of evidence that wet nurses, even at the lower levels of society, were expected to have a connection with their charges and adequately care for them. A woman named Breuga, who cared for a baby for the Hôpital du Saint-Esprit in 1434, had the infant removed from her care because she was unable to feed her properly (seemingly due to poverty rather than willful neglect); and across 150 years of the hospital's records there is only one instance of a woman looking after more than one child simultaneously.[50] It was clearly preferred that a woman devote all her time to one child, even if this meant more wet nurses needed to be found.

Although care for abandoned and orphaned children may have been undertaken by any available woman in a vicinity, the wet nurses of nobles and royals—and by the end of the Middle Ages, increasingly of mercantile and bourgeois classes—were selected far more carefully. Finding a suitable wet nurse was considered an art, and there were even manuscripts that helped couples understand the qualities that a wet nurse should possess. One such example is found in the writings of Italian physician Aldobrandino of Siena,

↙↙ As women were pushed out of practicing medicine, they managed to cling to one branch: serving as midwives during childbirth. In this depiction of the birth of Julius Caesar, a midwife pulls the baby from his mother while another woman pours water into a tub.

The Ancient History of the Romans (detail), fol. 219r, France (Paris), 1375–99 British Library, London; Royal MS 16 G VII

↙ Depictions of breastfeeding are surprisingly common in medieval art. Though such images usually show the Virgin Mary breastfeeding the Christ Child, there were secular depictions too, such as this woman feeding a baby while reclining in a bed.

Master of the Duke of Bedford (active c. 1405–1465), and others *Comédies de Térence*, fol. 230v, France (Paris), c. 1411 Bibliothèque Nationale de France, Paris; MS 664 réserve

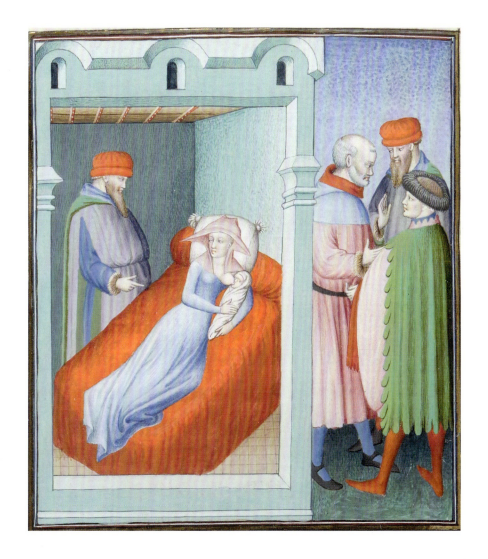

whose 1256 *Régime du corps* explains that one needed to consider a wet nurse's "age, her form, her habits, her breasts, whether she has good milk and whether the time since she had a child has been long or short," and of course her character, for this could travel through the milk and affect the character of the child. In these descriptions, wet nurses appear to have been examined almost as one might appraise an animal one was purchasing. Another medical text explains a wet nurse should not be blemished or have large, flabby breasts; instead, she should have "a large and ample chest," be "a little bit fat," and have a mixed complexion of white and redness.[51]

Wet nurses could find satisfaction in their roles beyond the monetary compensation. Some women became attached to the orphans that they fed through their first years of life and decided to adopt them, as was the case in 1313 of one Avenias and her husband, Bertran, who, after caring for an infant named Jomet for several months, asked to keep him as their own without any further payment for Avenias's wet-nurse services.[52] For wet nurses of the nobility, further employment could be had once the babies were weaned, as the women were often kept on in the household as nannies or governesses to the children until they were old enough to be taken under the wing of tutors. These wet nurses could also receive extra rewards from the parents, or even from the children themselves as they grew up, in the form of monetary gifts or donations of goods or even lands if they had remained in service with the family for many years.

Across the five centuries that we have looked at, women in Europe experienced huge changes. As the millennium began, peasant women were largely active in small, local jobs that supported their families. They worked at home and on the farm in rural areas, picking up small jobs supplementary to their everyday tasks in order to bring in additional income. They cared for animals, they cooked, they brewed ale, and they spun and sewed. But as the middle of the fourteenth century arrived, change was afoot. The Black Death transformed the face of Europe, contributing to a migration of people to growing urban centers and bringing a greater need for women to work. Advances in crafts and trades brought new skills and new opportunities to men and women alike, and the determination of medieval society to have businesses run by families meant that women had ample opportunity to develop their own expertise as they worked alongside their fathers and husbands. Women were so vital to this system that widows were often expected to continue the work of their husbands after their deaths, and they could be punished if they did not do so.

A real north–south divide existed in Europe with this emerging mercantile class. Women of the south faced stronger societal expectations to remain at home and act only as wives and mothers, meaning professional women emerged far more frequently in northern and western Europe. These professional women truly contributed to the emergence of this new class in society, bringing in plenty of wealth and status by their own merit and finding themselves more highly educated and skilled than their predecessors. But as

the medieval period drew to an end, this independence was severely tested. The emergence of guilds, licensing, and professionalization favored the participation of men in the workforce, and women increasingly found themselves pushed to the margins of the home once more. Female-dominated industries were taken over by men, and the expectations for peasant and professional women looked very different as the world headed into the early modern period.

II. RELIGIOUS WOMEN

During the Middle Ages, Christianity became the dominant religion in Europe. Though the Catholic Church was controlled by men in all the upper echelons, women still found plenty of space in which to express their religious devotion. Significant change in the landscape of Christianity in Europe transformed its accessibility to women during our period. The middle of the eleventh century saw the Great Schism, a series of fundamental disagreements in theology and how the church should be run that separated the church, once a united body, into Roman Catholicism and Eastern Orthodoxy. Most of the countries we are discussing were Roman Catholic, and so that branch of Christianity will be the focus of this chapter, but it is important to remember that women living on the eastern edges of Europe would have been under the sphere of the Orthodox church and may have had differing experiences than those in the west.

After the Great Schism, monumental discussions continued across Europe about how the church should be run, what doctrines should be adhered to, and other significant theological issues. The church was not a static entity, unchanging and clinging to tradition, and in fact, many developments occurred amid hopes of improving the church across its sphere of influence. The path was not always smooth, and from 1378 to 1417, the Papal Schism saw multiple claimants to the papacy, with rival popes residing in Rome, Pisa, and Avignon.

Even as this conflict persisted, members of the church who were dedicated to their religion remained determined to improve the world around them and live a religious life that aligned with their morals, beliefs, and worldview. The twelfth and thirteenth centuries, in particular, saw a huge religious revival across Roman Catholic Europe that would change access to the church for women. While women had always been part of the church, and indeed play a central role in the Bible, in the earlier medieval period true opportunities within the church were limited for women. Particularly holy and revered women could become saints, and various nobles and royals established a handful of nunneries for women who wanted to dedicate their lives to the church. These nunneries were not particularly numerous, however, and membership was often limited to royal and noble women whose familial connections and wealth could sustain the institutions.

During these two centuries, things began to change when male church members established new religious orders—some of the

Treatises, fol. 6v, France, c. 1290
Detail of page 81

→ Though the church was often dominated by men, religious women had plenty of female role models to guide them. The Virgin Mary was a role model for all women in medieval Europe, but she held a particular importance for religious women. They would have been surrounded by devotional images of Mary, such as this psalter that contains an illustration of the Nativity.

Psalter (detail), fol. 10v, Belgium (Bruges), 13th century
Getty, Los Angeles; Ms. 14

↘ While many images of the Virgin Mary depict her as a serene, faultless, and glorious woman, others show her more human side. This sculpture of Mary with the infant Jesus has echoes of ordinary medieval life. Although the symbolism of Mary holding a thornless rose and Jesus clasping an apple was intended to show that they both combated the sins of the world introduced by Adam and Eve, they are also an ordinary mother and child. This statue was thus an ideal that nuns could aspire to—that holiness was within their reach.

Virgin and Child with an Apple and a Rose, Germany, c. 1350–75
Ivory statuette with silver, gilt, and translucent enamel base, 3⅞ × 2⅞ in. (9.8 × 7.3 cm)
Metropolitan Museum of Art, New York

→→ Like the Virgin Mary, Eve was a popular biblical figure depicted in churches and manuscripts—in contrast, she was not someone nuns were encouraged to emulate. This manuscript illustration depicts Adam and Eve in the Garden of Eden. Eve is being tempted by the serpent, who remarkably is depicted with the face of a woman. This kind of depiction, seen in numerous forms of art, strengthens the notion that women were more easily led into temptation than men.

Willem Vrelant (d. 1481)
Book of hours, fol. 137r, Belgium (Bruges), c. 1460
Getty, Los Angeles; Ms. Ludwig IX 8

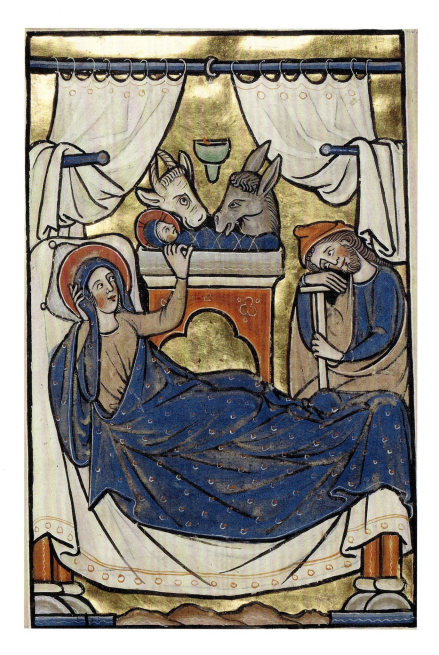

largest becoming the Benedictines, Franciscans, and Cistercians—
that were usually quick to admit women into their ranks. The orders were established as a way for people to live religious lives that
closely aligned with their beliefs and allowed them to demonstrate
their faith and piety through poverty, isolation, working the land,
or charity. Religious fervor spread through Europe as the transfor-
mations in the church and its organization were usually seen as
positive steps. Women were drawn into this revival too, often following pioneering monks on the front lines; the Dominican order
was founded by Dominic de Guzmán in 1206, when he established a
convent in France to house several of his female followers, meaning
the nuns of the order predated its monks.[1]

These centuries, therefore, saw an explosion in the number of
nunneries across Europe, and certain orders became just as popular

→ Female patrons of religious institutions were sometimes honored in art created by the convent, and the patron might decide to retire to the institution she supported. This frontispiece for *The Rule of Saint Augustine and the Constitutions of the Hospital of Notre-Dame of Seclin* depicts the hospital's founder, Marguerite II of Flanders, who is shown kneeling before Christ and surrounded by nuns. Marguerite is crowned and wearing a nun's habit, even though she did not take religious vows.

Master of the Golden Fleece of Vienna and Copenhagen (active 1460/70–1480)
The Rule of Saint Augustine and the Constitutions of the Hospital of Notre-Dame of Seclin, fol. 1r, France, 1470–80
Vieil Hôpital de Notre-Dame Archives, Seclin, France

↓ Though nuns often show up in manuscript art, they are less likely to appear as statues or objects. This reliquary depicts a Benedictine nun, and may represent Saint Scholastica, founder of the Benedictine nuns in the sixth century.

Reliquary bust, southern Netherlands/Belgium or northern France, c. 1500
Painted wood with gilding, 23⅝ × 16¾ × 13 in. (60.2 × 42.7 × 33 cm)
Philadelphia Museum of Art

among women as men. The Cistercian order was founded in the closing years of the eleventh century, expanded rapidly through the next century, and during the first half of the thirteenth century established a remarkable number of religious institutions for women. By 1300, the number of houses of Cistercian nuns and their male counterparts were almost equal, a trend seen across Europe and in other orders as well.[2] The majority of Ireland's nunneries were founded in the twelfth century, while just across the water in England, the same century saw the foundation of over one hundred houses for women, in stark contrast to the mere nine houses that existed prior to the Norman Conquest of 1066.[3] Medieval Iceland's two convents were founded during the twelfth and thirteenth centuries. In Germany, the nunnery of Engelthal, a famous European center of religious life, was founded in 1240 and became so popular it spawned a daughter house in 1269, and that daughter house in turn created its own daughter house a few decades later, in 1295.[4] Daughter houses, which formed when an institution could not fit any more nuns, remained under the control of the mother house, essentially acting as building extensions in different locations.

Between the creation of new orders and the endless founding of nunneries, women in the Middle Ages began to find that their options

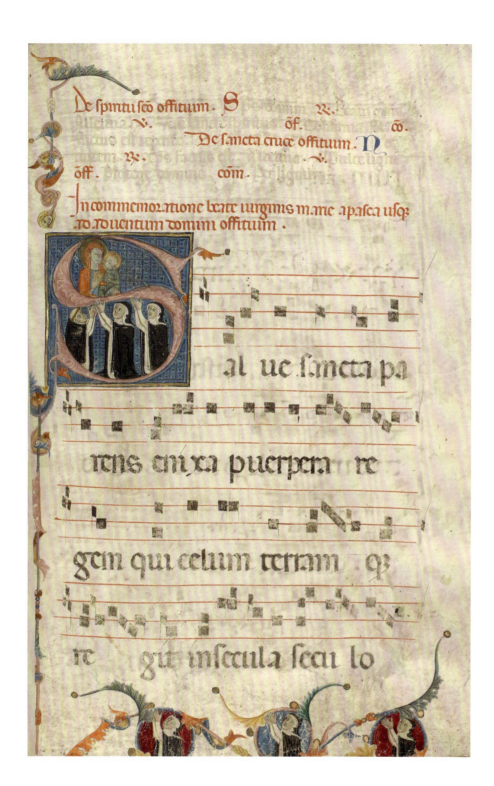

The historiated initial *S* on this page features the Virgin and Child above two Dominican nuns and a friar in prayer, while three more nuns offer up their prayers at the bottom. They decorate a page of a thirteenth-century gradual, a book containing the music sung during Mass.

Jacobellus of Salerno (active c. 1270)
Gradual, Italy (Bologna), fol. 70r,
c. 1270
Getty, Los Angeles; Ms. Ludwig VI 1

had greatly increased. No longer did one have to be a high-status woman relegated to choose among only a handful of houses; now membership opened to the knightly classes and later to the mercantile or bourgeois families who emerged at the end of the Middle Ages. Women could choose where they wanted to take their vows, finding a convent that aligned with their interests and beliefs, and surrounding themselves with like-minded women. If they couldn't find an establishment that they liked, they could start one of their own, as Bridget of Sweden did in the fourteenth century, founding the Bridgettines.

BECOMING A NUN

There was, therefore, plenty of choice as our period progressed for women who wanted to take the cloth and dedicate their lives to God. But why would a woman want to embark on a religious life in the first place, and how much was it her personal choice? For many years, it was assumed that women who became nuns were superfluous daughters, or women who needed to be hidden away to avoid bringing scandal to a family, or otherwise "inconvenient" women. While there were those cases, most of the evidence suggests life as a nun was considered a desirable life step—for the woman, her kin, and the wider community.

Not all women chose to join a nunnery. Many families did specifically select children—both male and female—for religious orders, sending them at a young age to begin learning the necessary skills to take their vows when they came of consenting age. But rather than a means of getting rid of unwanted children, it was considered an honor for the child to be chosen for religious life. For those of the lower ranks of society, a career in the church was a way to become educated and hold power that might otherwise elude them. For women in particular, becoming a nun held huge social obligation. As a nun, a woman was responsible for praying for souls who were stuck in purgatory before being allowed access to heaven. A woman was also expected to pray for the souls of her family, her ancestors, her institution's patrons and donors and their families, local leaders and royal families, and the world as a whole.[5] A nun's prayer was a powerful currency, and by entering the church, a woman took on a significant duty.

The church was open to women at all stages of life, and it was not only children who were sent to religious centers. Young women could decide to enter, and many saw the church as a preferable

alternative to marriage. Biographies, called *vitae*, or "lives," of female saints from the Middle Ages often include a story of a woman looking to join the church instead of marrying a man. One such woman was Theodora, who lived in England in the first half of the twelfth century. Theodora was a daughter in a wealthy family who, though believing to have spoken directly to Jesus at a young age and taken a personal vow of chastity, was beset by suitors, including a bishop who arranged a marriage for her in revenge after she rebuffed his sexual advances. Theodora fended off her betrothed, first by hiding and then by discussing religion with him, until she could be rescued by a hermit who took her to an anchoress. She then changed her name to Christina and ended up becoming a hermit at Markyate, near Saint Albans Abbey, where she became famous for her religious visions and later took her vows as a nun.[6]

For Christina of Markyate, religion was both vocation and escape from a life planned by others. Escape from the outside world certainly seems to have been an appealing aspect of taking religious vows for some women. Although written for those who had already taken their vows, the *Hali Meiðhad* (Holy maidenhood) sermon, composed in the late twelfth century, outlines the horrors of marriage, in which women are beaten, forced to have sex with men who "pursue filthiness at all times," and must undertake the endless and exhausting tasks of a housewife—including pregnancy and housekeeping.[7] An eleventh-century archbishop of Canterbury, Lanfranc, acknowledged that a motivation for many women in England who sought refuge as nuns was to escape the "libido" of the conquering Normans.[8] By becoming nuns, women avoided the disrespect shown to their married lay sisters and also guaranteed themselves the highest place in heaven, which was reserved for virgins.

While many women entered the religious life as children or

A stained glass window showing Saint Catherine reading a book and holding a sword. Women saints were perfect role models for nuns, and images of saints adorned their convents as reminders of ideal behavior and dedication to God.

Window of Saint Catherine, northern Netherlands, c. 1475
Stained glass, 36¼ × 22¾ in. (92 × 58 cm)
Rijksmuseum, Amsterdam

Christina of Markyate escaped an unwanted marriage by joining the church. She was a highly revered holy woman in England, and the exquisitely decorated Saint Albans Psalter is thought to have been made for her. Within the pages is this image of a woman, thought to be a portrait of Christina, and a group of monks approaching Christ.

Saint Albans Psalter, fol. 285r, England, 1120–45
Dombibliothek Hildesheim, Germany; HS St.God. 1

young adults, marriage did not prevent women from accessing the church. Wives were allowed to give up their marriage and join the church as nuns—though, crucially, they needed the consent of their husband to dissolve the marriage. Although this was a potential way for a couple to end an unhappy union, the husband was forbidden to remarry while his wife lived, and so, sending an unwanted wife to a nunnery did not result in a completely free man. Nonetheless, many marriages were dissolved in this way, such as that of Florentine noble Camilla Bartolini, whose husband allowed her to leave their marriage so that she could gather a group of women around her and found the convent of Saint Catherine of Siena in 1496.[9]

There are also plenty of examples of a married couple choosing to enter the religious life together, amicably parting ways as husband and wife to take up lives dedicated to God. In some parts of Europe, entire families even turned to a religious life. Around 1160, Peter of Veyrières joined the abbey of Obazine in France alongside his wife, sons, daughters, brother, and sister, the family donating its fortified house and entire estate to the abbey to support its upkeep.[10]

Widowhood provided the final opportunity for women to enter a convent. In the Middle Ages, widowhood could come at any age, even in childhood, and it was not unusual for widows to remarry— once or multiple times. Some women were happy to do this, but for others, the life of a nun provided an appealing alternative. There were several reasons a widow may have taken religious vows. If she had always wanted to live as a nun but had followed family and so- cial pressure to marry, having fulfilled this duty, she was now free to

monachis clementia ihu;

pursue the religious life. It might be that the woman did not necessarily wish to become a nun, but she did not want to be forced to remarry against her will, and taking the veil was a way to retain some freedom. An elderly widow who had spent decades as a wife and mother may have wanted some quiet holy reflection in her twilight years. She may have wanted to atone for her sins and those of her family, and took on the mantle of responsibility of saving their souls through her prayers. She may have simply wanted to be surrounded by a community of women now that she was no longer a wife, with the kinship that brought. Families often had an immediate member or an extended relative in the cloth, and taking religious vows may have been a chance to join a sister, mother, aunt, or cousin in her convent. For these reasons and for many more, medieval women became an official part of the church in their widowhood.

LIFE AS A NUN

When a woman, of any age and for any reason, decided to embark on a religious life, there were many considerations. The first was to pick an institution administered by an order with which the woman identified. The choice of order and institution would significantly impact her daily life. The rule of the Benedictines, for example, divided an individual's time into three categories: manual labor, spiritual reading, and prayer. Women who joined the Benedictine order were expected to read and to work, whether that was farming, cleaning, cooking, sewing, writing, or doing any other appropriate tasks. The Cistercians, meanwhile, tended to prefer physical isolation in the countryside, where members of the order could undertake spiritual contemplation without disturbance. Other orders prioritized working in the heart of a community to provide charity and care for the sick. Women of the Premonstratensian order did not undertake pastoral duties and were not expected to pray, and so they were usually uneducated. Other institutions highly valued education, such as Admont monastery in Austria, which operated a school to teach its nuns.[11]

The common thread connecting most medieval nunneries in Europe was a vow of poverty. Female houses were consistently poorer and had fewer assets than their male counterparts, and this was attributable to an expectation that their function differed from that of male institutions, rather than to their being less favored. Convents and monasteries of women were focused on their local community, and they existed to distribute charity and pray for those around them. Male institutions, by contrast, were often designed to be centers of learning and grand monuments to the glory of God, as well as seats for bishops and other high-ranking members of the church.

This does not mean that there were no wealthy female houses—there were certainly institutions in every country that were favored by the elite and wealthy. Some houses were laxer in their enforcement of poverty, and some places flouted rules altogether. A thirteenth-century archbishop of Rouen, Eudes Rigaud, visited many nunneries under his care, and scandalized by the nuns' behavior, he

Nuns had prescribed daily routines that revolved around prayer. These two nuns are shown sitting in a bare convent cell, one reading from a prayer book and the other holding a rosary.

Master of the Amsterdam Cabinet (active c. 1470–1500)
Two Nuns, Germany, 1478–82
Drypoint on paper, 3⅞ × 3⅛ in.
(9.9 × 7.9 cm)
Rijksmuseum, Amsterdam; RP-P-OB-930

reported on the rule breakers, citing those at Saint-Amand in Rouen, who slept on featherbeds and wore cloaks of rabbit; women at Notre-Dame d'Almenêches, who had necklaces; and those at Montivilliers, who wore peach-colored cloth and elaborate metal belts.[12]

Despite some women flouting the lifestyle of poverty, in parts of Europe, others were rushing to embrace the simple religious life. In thirteenth-century Italy, women used radical poverty as a tool to strike against the establishment. For many years, religious houses had been a means for local families to consolidate their secular power and enhance their riches. Nunneries were almost exclusively the preserve of noblewomen because a significant dowry was required for admission. Now, however, women of all social statuses decided to come together to live in communal poverty, regardless of their class or background in life (though the higher-status women still tended to hold the most power).

By eschewing their family's wealth, these women were freeing themselves from pressure and expectations outside the nunnery, ultimately affecting their lives within. They could follow their own choices, and this was, surprisingly, supported by some Italian religious men who helped these communities gain permission to exist outside of local ecclesiastical authority. These institutions thus became free of even the control of men—but strict conditions were imposed on this freedom. When Ugolino di Conti of Ostia, a previous supporter of these communities of poor religious women, became Pope Gregory IX in 1227, he created a *forma vitae*, or "way of life," for these groups that gave them great freedom in their monasteries. In return, however, the women had to strictly observe enclosure, never leaving their houses, interacting with the outside world only through a grill, and spending most of their days and nights in prayer. This reflected the kind of support Ugolino had shown to groups of religious women in Siena and Lucca as a papal legate, where he did so under condition that they were to hold no possessions and receive no income, living in dedication to their vows of poverty. If they broke these conditions, they would return to normal ecclesiastical jurisdiction, meaning male members of the church could dictate how they were to spend their days, and they would lose much of their autonomy.[13]

Overall, wherever one was in Europe, the life of a nun was expected to be simple. Many convocations of the church and its various religious orders spent time prescribing the life and duties of a nun. Women were expected to give up their worldly goods when they took the veil, using only what the church provided for them and what was shared among their fellow nuns. There was not supposed to be a hierarchy within a convent, and all the sisters were to have the same clothes, food, and accommodation. They were not to wear jewelry beyond the ring they were bestowed upon taking their vows, and their clothing should be plain but distinctive to their individual order. They would wear tunics or frocks with a cowl, wimple, and veil, keeping their foreheads covered down to their eyebrows. The fabrics were plain, and fur was not allowed. Their hair was to be styled simply. Generally, they were not allowed a pet, although some statutes permitted a nun to have a cat.[14] This uniformity among religious women is reflected in the art depicting nuns. Most images of nuns are of a staple design, showing a woman with a black dress and white undergarments. Some orders had slightly different accessories, like the nun's crown that became popular in some areas, and this could distinguish particular groups in period artworks. Most of the time, though, a nun was an immediately recognizable figure on any canvas.

The daily life of a woman in a religious order would vary based on her location in Europe, her rank within the institution, her role, the season, and so on. But there were general tasks a woman could expect to undertake regularly once she took her vows. Most women entered convents in which life was dedicated to prayer and work. They would have daily meetings where they could discuss scripture, talk about their sins and struggles, and organize the daily running of their house. They would be expected to attend Mass, read the Bible and other religious texts, pray by themselves or with a priest, and contemplate the state of their spirit. Their days were divided by

↑ Nuns were not supposed to have pets, as it was thought this would encourage them to care too much for worldly things. This scene from the *Life of Saint Hedwig* shows the saint discovering a pet hedgehog hidden in the sleeve of a bashful nun.

Life of Saint Hedwig (detail), fol. 70v, Poland (Silesia), 1353
Getty, Los Angeles; Ms. Ludwig XI 7

↗ Nuns undertook work alongside their prayers to keep them from idleness and thus temptation to sin. They commonly engaged in textile work, and this image shows a nun attempting to spin her distaff as she is humorously interrupted by a cat, one of the few animals nuns were sometimes allowed to keep as pets.

Maastricht Hours (detail), fol. 34r, Netherlands (Liège), 1300–1325
British Library, London; Stowe MS 17

canonical hours of prayer that dictated when they needed to partake in particular prayers or religious observances, fitting the rest of their daily tasks around these hours.[15]

Though convents employed laypeople to help with a multitude of tasks required to sustain the nuns, the nuns were often expected to get their hands dirty and help themselves. They had to cook, clean, do their washing, and darn their clothes. While some orders found it distasteful for nuns to undertake agricultural work, many nunneries across Europe engaged in animal husbandry and were supported by raising animals. The nuns would milk cows and sheep, produce butter and cheese, and clean and spin wool.

Many religious houses ran hospitals to care for the sick. Though modern ideas of a public health service were far away, it was recognized that society needed a way to care for those who fell ill. Towns and villages would have healers and doctors, but the church, as shepherd for the spiritual health of its people, became a natural place to care for their physical health as well. Furthermore, it was usually those within the church who had the access and opportunity to become educated in medical knowledge. Monks and nuns were, therefore, well equipped to be health-care providers.

Women were considered just as capable of caring for the sick and understanding medicine as men—in fact, it was expected that women who were wives and mothers would be knowledgeable about the uses of herbs and plants, and this extended to their religious sisters. It was a common trope in medieval poetry and romances for a woman to heal the male heroes and hold medical knowledge, such as in the story of Tristan and Iseult, in which the queen of Ireland is described as having unrivaled skills: "In all the world physician was there none so knowing of all manner and arts of healing, for she knew how to help all manner of diseases and wounds wherewith men be visited."[16]

From queens to peasants, women in the Middle Ages were expected to have some knowledge of medicine. It was assumed that women living in convents, with tomes of medical information at their fingertips, would be even more skillful. Nunneries across Europe created hospital wings in their complexes for their sisters to work in when they were not praying, and these hospitals also doubled as almshouses to care for the poor. The sisters of the Hôtel-Dieu at Laon washed visitors, brought disinfected water to pilgrims, and prepared food for their patients. The medical skills of nuns were not limited to taking care of the poor, who would have had few alternatives; one French chronicler records the time when King Louis IX was nearing death in Paris, and two women tended and nursed him back to health. It is thought that these women may have been nuns, which shows that even powerful monarchs relied on their wisdom. Nuns were not just passive distributors of medicine, as many turned their hand to disseminating the knowledge they had gained over their careers. Hildegard of Bingen, a famous German abbess of the twelfth century, wrote numerous medical and scientific texts, for which she was as highly respected as men of her time.[17]

While convents and abbeys provided an opportunity for religious women to gather together in a community, much of a woman's day would have been spent in silence and solitude. From wandering the cloister's gardens in meditation to sitting in her cell in private prayer, her day was largely dedicated to silent reflection. Silence was next to godliness, and it was normal for meals to be eaten without speaking, save for select sisters who would read religious texts aloud for the nuns to contemplate, nourishing their souls alongside their bodies. For many religious orders, leisure time was seen as a weakness that could encourage sin, and work and prayer were the only suitable activities to fill one's day.

Nuns distributed medicine and health care to those who came to their hospitals. In this scene depicting the Hôtel-Dieu, a hospital run by nuns in Paris, a novice is being welcomed (*left*) while a sick patient is being carried into another entrance (*right*). One nun waits with a key to receive the patient, and in the background, two sisters hang up sheets to dry. This manuscript illustration demonstrates just a few of the many tasks nuns performed in a hospital.

Jehan Henry, *Book of the Active Life at the Hôtel-Dieu of Paris*, fol. 15r, France, 1482 -83
Musée de l'Assistance Publique, Paris;
Ms. AP 572

ANCHORESSES AND BEGUINES

Though many women who entered the religious life became nuns, there were nuanced positions within the church and options to choose from, even for women. Some women chose to become an anchoress, a holy woman attached to a church, convent, or monastery who led a more intense life of seclusion than her fellow nuns. Anchoresses were enclosed in cells attached to a religious building and were expected to stay in these cells and not leave them. Decades of their lives could be spent in these rooms, and while they could be comfortably furnished, many were not very luxurious and measured only a few square feet in size. These women were sometimes kept company by other anchoresses, or could be visited by guests, and some had servants to care for them. Some anchoresses, however, had their only contact with the outside world through a window, where they could receive food and drink, hear sermons from priests, and speak to visitors.

While this lifestyle may seem difficult to our modern senses, the medieval world held anchoresses in high regard. They were not

Nuns were considered capable of running hospitals because of their learning and their spiritual authority. From a book instructing nuns in the "active life," this picture of nuns caring for sick patients at the Hôtel-Dieu in Paris is an allegory for not just physical sickness but spiritual sickness, which the nuns could also address. The four large nuns in black represent Prudence, Temperance, Fortitude, and Justice. While caring for the sick they are also instructing novices (women who had taken their vows but not completed apprenticeships) and "white girls," who were newly recruited but had not yet taken their vows.

Jehan Henry, *Book of the Active Life at the Hôtel-Dieu of Paris*, fol. 167r, France, 1482–83
Musée de l'Assistance Publique, Paris; Ms. AP 572

inferior to their male counterparts (anchorites), and as with nuns praying for the souls of the dead, anchoresses fulfilled a vitally important role in society. The *Ancrene Riwle*, an early thirteenth-century guidebook for anchoresses, explained that these women gained their names because they were "anchored under a church like an anchor under the side of a ship to hold it so that the waves and the storm do not pitch it over. So all Holy Church which is called a ship, shall be anchored to the anchoress and she shall hold it secure so that the puffing and blowing of the devil . . . do not pitch it over."[18] Women who chose to live as an anchoress were protecting the souls of the world around them with their work, saving humanity from its sins. People at all levels of society, from peasants to emperors, would give money to anchoresses as a general assurance for their soul and also at times of need, such as during sickness or if there was a threat to the life of the king.

The appeal of becoming an anchoress came, in part, from the equal opportunity it presented for women from all ranks. There were few barriers to becoming an anchoress; aspirants could be young or old, virgins or widows, women who had seen much of the world or women who had seen little of it, and even women who were not already nuns. In the early eleventh century, an Icelandic woman named Guðríður Þor-bjarnardóttir undertook a pilgrimage all the way to Rome. Inspired by her journey, she appears to have taken vows, for when she returned to Iceland she became an anchoress on her farm.[19] It didn't matter that she had no prior experience of a religious life.

Becoming an anchoress was a popular choice for medieval European women, and in many countries anchoresses far outnumbered anchorites. Anchoresses were venerated in their local communities, earning saintlike reputations and being sought for their

Anchoresses were shut away, but they still were able to have some interaction with the outside world through windows in their rooms. This manuscript illustration shows Arthurian knight Perceval meeting with his aunt, who had once been a queen but was now an anchoress. Anchoresses would bestow wisdom and teach visitors about Christianity through these windows.

The Quest for the Holy Grail and the Death of Arthur (detail), fol. 21v, France, 1380–85
Bibliothèque Nationale de France, Paris; Français 343

Anchoresses were highly revered for their wisdom and holiness. This image shows a king consulting an anchoress—even the most powerful men in Europe were happy to submit to the authority and advice of a religious woman.

Rothschild Canticles, fol. 118r, Flanders or Rhineland, c. 1300
Yale University Library, New Haven, CT; Beinecke MS 404

When women became anchoresses, they underwent a solemn ceremony as they were sealed off from the world. This image shows a bishop blessing and enclosing an anchoress within her cell.

Pontificale, fol. 96r, England, 1400–1410
Corpus Christi College, Cambridge, England; MS 79

Anchoresses were often bricked up into their cells, firmly shutting them away from the world as if they were dead. In this manuscript image, Jephthah's daughter is being walled in like a recluse. In the biblical story, Jephthah accidentally offers the life of his daughter to God. In some interpretations, Jephthah was forced to kill his daughter, but others say that she was offered religiously and spent the rest of her life in seclusion, like a medieval anchoress.

Pamplona Bible (detail), fol. 73v, Spain, 1197
Amiens Municipal Library, France; BM, 0108

advice and the power of their prayers. They spent their days in quiet seclusion, reading and praying. But one could not simply decide to become an anchoress. It was quite a task for an institution to maintain an anchoress. She had to be cared for, brought food and drink, have her washing done, and a priest would have to come to hear confession, pray, and give the Eucharist. Anchoresses were highly sought positions, and while it was possible for new anchoresses and cells to be created, a woman often had to wait for a current anchoress to die, or occasionally move to another institution, so that she could take her place.

This meant that while the opportunity to become an anchoress was open to anyone, many places had a stringent process for all women wishing to take the vows, and over time, a ritualized ceremony took shape for officially admitting an anchoress. An aspirant's faith would be tested by her local church leaders—a bishop or archbishop. A special service was held in the church where she would be embarking on her new life, with blessings and readings given before the anchoress was taken to her cell, sprinkled with dust, and enclosed. The sprinkling of dust represented the idea that anchoresses were essentially considered dead to society. Most anchoresses would not emerge from their cells alive; they were wholly under the care of the church they were attached to, their entire being dedicated to prayer and God.

If becoming an anchoress seemed a step too far for a woman wishing to join the church, there were less dedicated roles that she could inhabit instead. Around the time of the religious revival of the twelfth and thirteenth centuries, a new movement spread among northern European women. Some women longed to live similarly

to nuns, undertaking a life of poverty and dedicating their time to prayer, but for various reasons they did not wish to take the actual vows of a nun. These women started to gather in groups of like-minded people and form communities in towns where they could live according to their vision. They became known as beguines, living lives of self-sufficiency, unbeholden to the rules of a particular order unless they chose otherwise.

Being outside of the church, beguines were exempt from answering to men, unlike communities of nuns. Not having taken vows, they retained more personal freedom, being able to live close to towns, travel as they desired, and work to support themselves. The concept of groups of single women living together and not under the control of a man was subversive to the natural order of society, and initially these groups met strong resistance from the church; in the early 1300s, Pope Clement V ordered that any such community be suppressed, going so far as to call the beguines heretics.

But from the start, beguines found strong backing among powerful laypeople who were happy to lend their support. In the thirteenth century, the Countesses of Flanders, Jeanne and Margaret, both established and endowed numerous beguine groups in their territories, while King Louis IX of France created many beguinages across France, including a significant one in Paris in 1264 that could house four hundred inhabitants.[20] Contemporary writing explains that the support for these groups came from an understanding that some women were too poor to find suitable marriages, and beguinages gave them an opportunity to support themselves respectably—but these societies also recognized that many who became beguines were in fact noblewomen.

Noble beguines may have been women who could no longer support the excesses of their position and wanted to live more humbly, thus bringing them closer to God. One such woman was Adelheid Rotter, who had once been in the service of royals, traveling with Princess Elizabeth of Hungary to Thuringia to meet her betrothed. Despite living such a comfortable life, Adelheid decided she wanted to give up what she described as her "sinful life" to become a beguine in Nuremberg, eventually establishing the nearby nunnery of Engelthal.[21] Although they held an unofficial religious status, beguines were not necessarily seen as less devout than their avowed sisters. It was recognized that beguines also dedicated themselves to God and holiness and that they could have unique spiritual powers. Marie d'Oignies, a beguine who lived in Liège, France, at the turn of the thirteenth century, became renowned for protecting the souls of people on their deathbed from demons who tried to claim them.[22]

CLOISTERING AND MISBEHAVING

The concerns expressed by early critics of the beguine movement were ones that followed all religious women throughout the Middle Ages. While it was recognized that religious women performed a vital task for society, saving souls from purgatory and securing a woman's place in heaven, worries constantly circulated about the

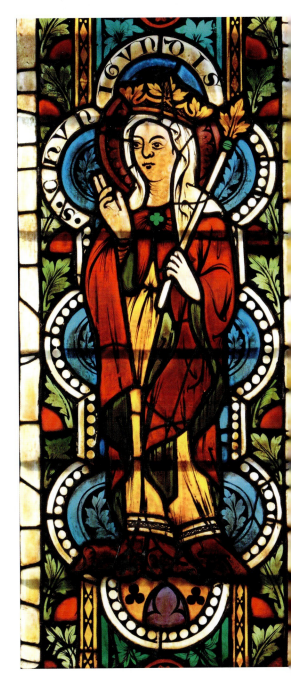

Secular women could turn to the church later in life and still gain renown for their piety. This stained glass window honors Kunigunde, who was Holy Roman empress in the early eleventh century, and posthumously attained sainthood. Noble and royal women who became revered for their holiness could serve as role models to nuns who were often noble and royal themselves.

Queen Kunigunde (detail), Austria, 1340–50
Stained glass panel, 38½ × 17½ in. (97.8 × 44.5 cm)
Metropolitan Museum of Art, Cloisters, New York

existence of large female communities outside of male control. Nunneries had to answer to male members of the church, who would undertake regular visitations to their institutions to ensure the nuns were following the rules of the order, and other female houses were physically situated alongside male ones in joint abbeys. But as the men overseeing the nuns perceived, the temptation to sin was always around the corner. Women were seen as the weaker sex, more prone to temptation and thus in need of protection lest they sin—or cause others to sin with them. A group of women gathering together, even within the church, must surely be a recipe for disaster.

Early on, a straightforward solution was found to reduce the chance for women to fall into temptation: cloistering. Also known as enclosure, this practice was based on the notion that religious women who had taken their vows should be sheltered from the rest of the world and live simply among other nuns with very few (or, ideally, no) visitors. By figuratively, or even literally, locking away nuns, the men of the church did not need to worry about the women's chastity being compromised.

The strictness of enclosure fluctuated over time and varied from region to region. Early in the period, the enclosure tended to be very literal, with walls built around the female religious houses, which were also often geographically isolated. During the twelfth century, the nuns of the joint monastery of Admont in Austria were sealed in their cloisters by a door with three locks, which was opened only when a new nun joined or when one inside died. This proved almost

↑ Virginity was highly prized in medieval Europe, and virgins were thought to have the highest place in heaven. This painting, made for a nunnery in Florence, where it would have had central importance, shows part of the legend of the martyrdom of Saint Ursula and eleven thousand virgins. The scene would have reassured the convent's nuns of their place in heaven as women who had dedicated themselves to God.

Bernardo Daddi (active c. 1312–1348)
Arrival of Saint Ursula at Cologne, Italy (Florence), c. 1333
Tempera and gold leaf on triptych panel,
26 × 26¾ in. (66 × 67.9 cm)
Getty, Los Angeles

→→ Nuns were not always segregated by their gender. In this manuscript miniature, monks and nuns attend Mass and follow in a church procession. The nuns are active participants, as one woman rings the bells (*top*), and two others carry open books of music (*bottom*).

Treatises, fol. 6v, France, c. 1290
British Library, London;
Yates Thompson MS 11

disastrous in 1152, when a fire broke out in the male quarters and moved toward the women's buildings—the senior monk of the abbey could not find the two keys he was responsible for, and the door had to be broken down to save the women from burning to death.[23] Over time, rules tended to soften slightly to allow the women more movement, but the ideology of separating women from men remained strong. During the unavoidable times when a nun was to speak with a man, ideally it would be done through a window while she remained in the abbey with a mature companion alongside her.

This idea of separation became so insidious that it spread to all aspects of the nuns' lives. They eventually were given their own place in the church to listen to Mass, which they entered through their own door connected to their quarters. In many locations, this sequestering became so extreme that the nuns could not even see the altar during the service, so keen was the desire to shield them from the rest of the congregation. But women became frustrated with being cut off from such an essential part of their religion and began to fight back. For centuries in the Iberian Peninsula, women had been limited in how often they could take Communion, and

they were usually so sequestered away in the church that they could not see the Eucharist being performed. Eventually, it was conceded that it was important for women also to be afforded this view. The nuns started to gain limited power in other respects too, absorbing some of the responsibilities of their male counterparts, particularly if they were high status.[24]

With such strict rules for cloistering, it is unsurprising that communities such as the beguines grew in popularity with women who desired to express their faith and piety without being locked away from the world. But time and again, medieval men demonstrated that cloistering was their preference for dealing with religious women. In 1298, Pope Boniface VIII made enclosure compulsory for all Catholic nuns, making it law that nuns were not to leave their convents, and unlicensed outsiders were forbidden to enter. In this, he was following in the footsteps of his predecessor from the start of the century, Pope Innocent III, who had reorganized all the informal groups of holy women in Rome into cloistered communities.[25] This was in sharp contrast to priests and monks, who were free to travel as they pleased. Even if monks attached to monasteries might prefer to stay in the isolation of their institutions, there were no rules forbidding them from entering the world and interacting with others. In fact, this was often encouraged, as they might travel to preach, perform sacraments, or inspect female religious houses.

Despite the strict rules for enclosing nuns, many of the women who ran the nunneries had to leave the cloister on occasion. Abbesses and prioresses were important to local communities and could be summoned on business; they were also expected to advocate for the lands and rights that their house controlled, such as benefices, which allowed them to choose appointments to church positions, or income from tithes. This led to the need to leave the convent's protective walls, but even in these cases, the women usually had to obtain permission from the male supervisor of their institution and were expected to be chaperoned by other nuns or priests.[26] It is significant, though, that these abbesses were entrusted with such an important role. Recognized for their education, they could read the records relating to the management of their lands and were competent in administration and negotiation.

As can be expected of a populace bound by rules, many women broke them. Infractions could vary from an individual misbehaving nun to entire houses not engaging in correct, expected behavior. Toward the end of the Middle Ages, rules tended to be much more relaxed, but across Europe, countless convents took rule-breaking to the extreme, flouting what had once been a strictly implemented regime. Even the most revered of institutions could fall foul, such as the convent of Engelthal, which had essentially become a home for single noblewomen toward the end of our period. The cloister garden, once a place for prayer and contemplation, became a stable for horses, which the nuns scandalously rode for sport, leaving their compound walls and cavorting with men—and in several cases bearing children.[27]

Despite the strict enclosure rules, some nuns became pregnant.

In fact, the strictness of the cloistering meant that their impregnators were often religious men—priests and monks—because laymen had been so successfully kept away from the nuns. And being a high-ranking nun was no assurance that one would not commit this sin: in 1431 the convent of Reynistaðarklaustur in Iceland experienced scandal when two nuns became pregnant, one being the former subprioress and the other the daughter of the convent's steward. The father of one of the children was the convent's priest and confessor, a man given privileged access to these women, whose spiritual welfare he was supposed to be caring for. Two centuries earlier, Archbishop Eudes had recorded that in 1249, ten of the nineteen or so nuns of the Benedictine priory of Villarceaux were involved in sex scandals, and six of the nuns' sexual partners were also in holy orders.[28] Although such cases were a scandal for the church, those in the secular world sometimes found amusement in their acts—images of nuns behaving salaciously can often be found in the margins of manuscripts.

What happened to those who flouted the carefully agreed-upon rules of the Catholic Church? The church was hesitant to remove anyone who had taken sacred religious vows, which were considered binding until death, and anyone who fled the church after taking these oaths was cast among the most morally reprehensible in society. So, even if a nun had worn luxurious furs, had a baby, and shirked her duties, the church would not throw her out. Depending on the severity of the misdeed, the woman may have been disciplined within her own institution or sent to another where a closer eye could be kept on her. She would be made to undertake penances, focus her days on prayer, and atone for her sins in a variety of ways. Others were sent to undesirable locations, as was the case with a thirteenth-century nun near Rouen, France, who was forced to work in a leper house as punishment for helping another nun meet her lover and then assisting her with an abortion when the tryst inevitably led to an undesirable outcome.[29]

↖ Abbesses led communities of nuns within an abbey and were responsible for the welfare of the women in their care. This abbess teaching her fellow nuns decorates the initial letter *A*, for "Abbatissa" (abbess), within a medieval encyclopedia promising "all good things" (*Omne Bonum*).

Jacobus [James le Palmer], *Omne Bonum*, fol. 27r, England, 1360–75 British Library, London; Royal 6 E VI

↑ Not all nuns behaved impeccably. Many had improper relations with men, and some became pregnant as a result—a possible outcome of this nun's frolicking. This image was drawn by a female illuminator, Jeanne de Montbaston, who we will meet again in chapter IV.

Jeanne de Montbaston (active c. 1320–1355) Guillaume de Lorris and Jean de Meun, *Le Roman de la rose* (detail), fol. 111v, France, 14th century Bibliothèque Nationale de France, Paris; Français 25526

MYSTICS AND THEIR VISIONS

A phenomenon that became significant across parts of medieval Europe was the female mystic. The defining characteristic of a mystic was that she saw visions sent from heaven. She would witness and perhaps speak to Jesus Christ, the Virgin Mary, saints and angels, and deceased nuns. The visions gave her a direct line to God, helping her to understand the Bible and Christian ideology and theology. The visions could be prophetic, instructing a woman on changes that needed to happen around her or showing her a path to follow; or they could give the woman an insight into the past, where she might witness key biblical scenes like the birth of the Virgin Mary, the birth of Christ, or the Crucifixion.

Mysticism became closely entwined with femininity, as it was usually women who experienced these visions. Mystics were typically religious women who had already taken the cloth and had a deep knowledge of religion and a predisposition to be connected to God, but any woman could become a mystic after having a life-changing experience. These holy women were touched by God, but they could suffer from this connection. Female mystics could experience uncontrollable crying, be struck down by paralyzing illnesses, or have stigmata (wounds that correspond with the wounds Christ suffered on the cross) appear on their bodies.

Women seen as blessed with the gift of vision could ascend to a revered status in medieval Europe, and indeed some of them were canonized and raised to sainthood after their deaths. Even those who were not granted this great honor could find significant fame and respect during their lifetimes, with people traveling from far and wide to receive their wisdom. As the written word proliferated through the Middle Ages, these holy women were encouraged to write down their visions and work with a male confessor to organize their thoughts and insights into religious matters and life itself. Interestingly, mystics appear to have had input into the decoration of the manuscripts of their visions, and this gives us a unique opportunity to see into the minds of these women. It was common for the works to be illustrated with the women's visions—sometimes drawn by the mystic herself—and they show us not only the type of visions they were experiencing but how they wanted to portray them to others.

Hildegard of Bingen, the mystic mentioned earlier, was born in 1098 to noble parents and was always destined for a holy life. Her visions began early—she experienced her first before she was five years old—and at eight years old, she was sent to the monastery at Disibodenberg in Germany, where she was mentored by a respected anchoress named Jutta. After decades of living quietly as a nun, not sharing her visions with anyone beyond Jutta and a monk named Volmar, at the age of forty-two, she received a life-changing vision instructing her to write down her understanding of Christian texts. Hildegard was still unsure, but after receiving permission from the abbot of Disibodenberg, she finally started recording her visions. Word of her powers spread first to the archbishop of Mainz and finally to the pope.

The church was keen to verify the truth of Hildegard's mysticism,

← Mystics often had visions of important biblical events—this nun is shown witnessing the birth of the Virgin Mary.

Cutting from Dominican choir book (detail), leaf, Germany (probably Cologne), c. 1500
Victoria and Albert Museum, London; 2963

↓ This sculpture of Saint Anne after she gave birth to the Virgin Mary formed part of an altarpiece in a German parish church. Burn marks from candles indicate that it was worshiped as a devotional image.

Nativity of the Virgin, Germany, c. 1480
Limewood with paint, 14¼ × 54 × 17 in. (36.2 × 137.2 × 43.2 cm)
Metropolitan Museum of Art, Cloisters, New York

and in the late 1140s, a commission was sent to investigate her. Having been satisfied with the veracity of Hildegard's powers, the commission returned with a portion of her writings to Trier, Germany, where a synod was being held. The pope himself read her piece aloud to the assembled archbishops and cardinals—some of the most important men of the Catholic Church at the time—and all were struck with wonder at her words. The assembly commanded

Hildegard to continue to record anything that the Holy Spirit revealed to her; Hildegard's mysticism was now ordained not only by God but by the church, and this made her one of the most important figures of her day.

Hildegard's newfound fame brought an explosive popularity to her monastery, which was inundated with applications from women who wanted to become nuns just to live alongside Hildegard. But Hildegard received further visions that instructed her to establish her own nunnery, at Rupertsberg in Bingen, which later expanded to a second convent across the Rhine at Eibingen, to house the endless nuns who wanted to follow her. Everybody who was anybody wanted to hear from Hildegard, even royalty; she corresponded with King Frederick Barbarossa of Germany from the 1150s onward. She even had a rare honor of being allowed to publicly preach. For most of the history of Christianity, women had been discouraged, and even outright banned, from preaching. It was deemed that only men should and could be allowed to hold the authority to explain the Bible and the Word of God to the public. But Hildegard was thought to be touched by the Holy Spirit, and so her words came directly from heaven. She undertook a series of preaching tours across Germany, speaking not only to men and women of the cloth but also to the public, in 1160 in Trier.[30]

Hildegard was not the only mystic to find a home along the Rhine. As the Middle Ages progressed, German-speaking lands had a particularly high concentration of mystic nuns, most prominently, it seems, among women of the Dominican order. This may have

Elsbeth Stagel, *Lives of the Nuns of Töss* (detail), fol. 3r, Germany, 1459/60 Stadtbibliothek Nürnberg, Germany; Cod. Cent. V 10a

←← Although we know that many nuns were scribes and writers, they are not very often depicted in the act of writing in medieval art. This small illumination in the sister book of Töss Monastery shows Elsbeth Stagel writing her manuscript—a collection of biographies of thirty-nine nuns from her convent's history.

Elsbeth Stagel, *Lives of the Nuns of Töss* (detail), fol. 3r, Germany, 1459/60 Stadtbibliothek Nürnberg, Germany; Cod. Cent. V 10a

↙↙ Mystics were generally holy women who claimed to have visions sent to them from God and the heavens. This manuscript initial shows a vision received by a nun named Margaret von Zurich, who saw herself bathing the Christ Child. Margaret's vision was subversive despite its simplicity— women were forbidden by the church from touching Christ. The nuns of Saint Katherine's convent in Nuremberg, who created this image, were therefore undertaking a potentially dangerous act in recording it.

Elsbeth Stagel, *Lives of the Nuns of Töss* (detail), fol. 29r, Germany, 1459/60 Stadtbibliothek Nürnberg, Germany; Cent. V 10a

← Hildegard of Bingen received visions from God, and after much encouragement, she wrote them down (*bottom right*). This picture from a posthumous copy of one of her books shows her receiving a vision of the Trinity (God, Jesus Christ, and the Holy Spirit) and a fallen angel. She has a tablet in front of her, stylus in hand, ready to record what she sees. A monk sits writing, ready to copy her words.

Hildegard of Bingen, *The Book of Divine Works* (detail), fol. 1v, Italy, 1210–30 Biblioteca Statale di Lucca, Italy; MS 1942

been due to the importance the Dominicans placed on education. Dominican nuns were far more likely than nuns of other orders to be highly educated and able to read Latin, and they had access to many theological texts. Thus, they had deep understanding of the Bible and the intricacies of Christianity.[31]

Other regions in Europe were slower to pick up on the mysticism trend, but most if not all countries and territories claimed a mystic at some point in the Middle Ages. Mystics could be a powerful force for reform in regions that were crying out for it. If a woman's visions aligned with what regional members of the church wanted to reform, then the woman would be heralded for the truths she spoke, for she provided evidence that what the men were pushing for was correct.

But the mystic who pushed for reform had to be careful of what she said, because holy visions from God initially were treated with suspicion. Even Hildegard of Bingen was tested to make sure her visions were pure and not sent from the devil to tempt people to sin— or that they were not outright lies. The growing number of women claiming to be speaking with God could greatly benefit Christianity and the institutions they represented, but many such women were

←← This nun's crown, made by the nuns of Rupertsberg convent in Germany, is thought to have belonged to Hildegard of Bingen and was venerated as a relic because of her perceived holiness. Although wearing a crown became common among numerous orders of nuns, Hildegard's example is the only one from the Middle Ages to survive. The blue cap is a later addition meant to support and highlight the pale silk crown, which originally was worn over a nun's veil. Hildegard designed this crown for her nuns, but she had to defend the wearing of it to critics.

Crown of Hildegard von Bingen, Germany, 1170s and 1600s
Silk-band crown over blue velvet cap, height: 6⅝ in. (17 cm)
Abegg Stiftung Foundation, Riggisberg, Switzerland

↙↙ In this devotional triptych depicting the Crucifixion, a Bridgettine nun kneels in the foreground, her recognizable crown visible. An inscription at the nun's feet reads "S Filicita," most likely identifying her as Felicità di Francesco Casavecchia, who joined the Bridgettines in 1455, around the time the painting was created. This portable triptych might have therefore commemorated her entry into the order.

Paolo Uccello (1397–1475)
The Crucifixion, c. 1455
Tempera on wood, gold ground, 18 × 11 in. (45.7 × 27.9 cm)
Metropolitan Museum of Art, New York

← Nuns were generally expected to have enough literacy to read the Bible and other religious texts. This group of Dominican nuns in a church's choir is reading, possibly from hymnals.

Psalter of Henry VI, fol. 177v, France, c. 1420
British Library, London; Cotton Domitian A. XVII

greeted instead with fear, suspicion, or outright hatred. Augustinian prioress Alijt Bake in the city of Ghent in the Low Countries experienced this during the fifteenth century. Alijt held power as the leader of a convent, but during a church visitation in 1455, she was deposed from her position and exiled from the community, accused of corrupting the women in her care by encouraging the convent to reform through her visions.

It was clear that the men of the church saw Alijt as dangerous. They forbade the inmates of all the female institutions in the region from composing or copying any theological or mystical text altogether—not just the teachings of Alijt. This threat to their person was not lost on many female mystics. Hildegard had only started recording her visions under extreme encouragement, including from the pope himself. The fourteenth-century English mystic Julian of Norwich was clearly anxious that her visions could be misconstrued as heresy, as she was particularly careful about how she was perceived in her writings: in her *Revelations of Divine Love* she exclaims, "but God forbid

that you should say or take me for a teacher for I don't intend that nor ever did so, for I am a woman, ignorant, [weak] and frail."[32] For some female mystics, this danger resulted in the ultimate punishment. Marguerite Porete, a wandering preacher in France during the late 1200s and early 1300s, wrote *The Mirror of Simple Souls*, which explains the knowledge she had obtained through her visions. These visions led her to the conclusion that she did not need theological instruction or to receive the sacraments of the church because of her personal connection to God—a significant threat to the authority of the church. By 1306, her book was burned by the church in her presence, and she was warned to cease spreading her ideas. Marguerite attempted to gain legitimacy for her visions by sending the book to three theologians, who all approved her work, but despite this support, she was seen as too dangerous and was burned at the stake as a heretic in 1310.[33]

Though the life of a mystic could be dangerous, woman mystics in a region with a history of visionaries, or those with the support of male church members, could gain great power from their associated holiness. Most female mystics were encouraged to record their visions, usually with the help of a priest, and these texts circulated widely across Europe. It was not just fellow monks and nuns who were interested in what these mystics had to say; their teachings and writings were popular with laypeople too. Fifteenth-century Swiss mystic Magdalena Beutler left behind ninety-three known surviving manuscripts and printed books of her works, proof that her writings were widely disseminated. And in the previous century, a nun of Engelthal, Christina Ebner, received a visit from King Charles IV of Bohemia—later the Holy Roman emperor. He was accompanied by a bishop, three dukes, and numerous counts, who all "came and knelt down before her greatly desiring that she give them something to drink and a blessing."[34]

One of the Middle Ages' most famous mystics, a woman who defied convention in every aspect of her life, was Joan of Arc. In the fifteenth century, Joan leveraged the recently accepted role of mystic as adviser to the great and the good in an entirely new way. Although mystic women like Christina and Hildegard had corresponded with and met kings and leaders and provided advice, Joan went a step further and actively sought out the king of France for her mission. What was even more remarkable was that she was an obscure, uneducated peasant girl, not an educated nun, as many of the mystics who had previously filled this role had been.

Joan first heard a voice when she was thirteen, and over the course of her teenage years she discerned that she was able to hear from Saints Catherine and Margaret and the archangel Michael. She saw them multiple times a day, and they instructed her to save France from the English, who during the course of the Hundred Years' War, had taken much of their land and even claimed their kingship.[35] While Joan was ultimately condemned by the English as a heretic and witch and burned at the stake, to the French she helped lead to victory, she was a saint sent from God with a direct line to the heavens—whose holiness had been proven true time and again.

Joan of Arc is one of the most famous medieval women, known for her visions, her trailblazing role in turning the tides of the Hundred Years' War, and her fight against cultural norms for women. Although her story ultimately ended in tragedy, she gained a huge following during her life and beyond. Joan is one of the rare examples of a medieval woman depicted in battle (other depictions usually portray women from earlier history or myth); here she leads forces at the siege of Paris in 1429.

Jean Bourdichon (c. 1457–1521); circle of François Le Barbier (active c. 1460s–1480s)
Vigils of King Charles VII, fol. 66v, France, 1484–85
Bibliothèque Nationale de France, Paris; Français 5054

Joan became a popular figure depicted in art for the legendary status she managed to achieve in her lifetime. Manuscripts across Europe told the tale of the heroic maiden, and these were accompanied beautifully by images of Joan leading troops into battle. By the fifteenth century, there were already a multitude of compendiums that explored the lives of numerous extraordinary women from history, and Joan easily slotted in alongside them. Her appearance in artwork during the fifteenth century and beyond reflects her popularity and her uniqueness, and each new piece of art served only to bolster her reputation further.

POWER AND PEACE

A woman who was part of the church could hold much greater power than she may have had in secular life. Whether it was as a mystic who enthralled Europe with her visions, an anchoress who was responsible for the souls of her community, a prioress or abbess who was in charge of a whole community of women, or just an ordinary nun who nonetheless carried the heavy burden of praying for souls in purgatory—women were at the heart of the church. The power of these women extended beyond the doors of their communities and into the wider world. They held authority over not only the women in their care but the men around them too—a privilege women outside of the church were afforded only if they were of noble blood. Many powerful religious women were, of course, members of the nobility, but women from the knightly and mercantile classes could rise in social status through the church and continue their climb if they proved skillful enough.

It was common for nuns to join a local institution rather than travel across a country or abroad to join a religious house, though this did occur.[36] This meant that many women who symbolically eschewed the secular life by being sequestered away in a cloistered community still in fact retained familial ties outside the walls of their institutions. They would write to and sometimes see their relatives, and this left them with an investment in the outside world. It also meant they could continue to wield influence over lay society through the prestige of their position. They were even trusted by strangers in their community, as their holiness and dedication to God meant they were seen as impartial witnesses and arbitrators. For this reason, nuns often acted as executors of wills of laypeople or witnesses to resolutions. This was the case in 1217, when the abbess of Notre-Dame-aux-Nonnains in France placed her seal on the charter of a resolution of a dispute between a noble couple and their neighbor, showing her as the independent recorder of the agreement.[37]

Female religious houses also served as places of refuge for ordinary women in society. Women viewed these holy sites as places of sanctuary, somewhere they could be protected from the very real dangers outside their doors. In the late twelfth century, Pope Alexander III arbitrated in a case of a woman who had fled to a female monastery for protection when she was in danger of being killed by her husband. She sheltered in the monastery until her husband died, and then requested permission from the pope to leave the walls and remarry. The woman needed permission in this case, as the criteria for becoming a nun were surprisingly simple in the Middle Ages; any woman who wore religious clothes for a year was considered to have become a nun, even if she hadn't taken vows, and thus she was not free to leave the institution she had joined. Alexander gave the woman permission to depart on the proviso that fear of her husband had been her only motivation for entering the monastery. The protection of a convent could also be more temporary, as was the case of a woman in Laon, France, who sought safety among her local community of nuns while escaping a mob during a communal uprising in the city.[38]

The protection of a community of religious women did not extend just to those in immediate physical danger. Orphans could find homes in these institutions, but widows were a more frequent presence. Although many widows chose to take holy vows, others—particularly nobles—wanted the peace and safety of a convent without the restrictions of vows. For a noble or royal woman, a convent was somewhere she could live among the religious, have a reprieve from the demands of court, and live a much simpler life than she had outside the walls (though "simpler" did not always

Tab. XII.

Congregatio religiosa temporibus Rilindis et Herradis abbatum in diservicio Ihohenbure caritative adunata.

mean less luxurious as, not being a nun, she could take her worldly possessions with her).

Although the church would have preferred that some of these women take the cloth, it found a solution for women who wanted to enter the convent in this way: they could become vowesses. Many chose this option because it enabled them to have the best of both worlds. Vowesses were so named for the single vow they took upon entering these homes, which was one of chastity. The church worked extremely hard to protect the chastity of nuns, and it could not allow a laywoman to enter and ruin their efforts. After all, as twelfth-century nun Héloïse wrote in a letter to her husband, "surely nothing is so conducive to a woman's seduction as woman's flattery, nor does a woman pass on the foulness of a corrupted mind so readily to any but another woman; which is why St Jerome particularly exhorts women of a sacred calling to avoid contact with women of the world."[39]

By taking a vow of chastity, the vowess was reducing the potential for corruption within her institution. However, by not being a fully professed nun, she retained her personal freedom. She could continue to own property, wear luxurious clothes and jewels, eat pleasant food, and, importantly, leave the convent to go about her business in the secular world as she pleased. While many wealthy widows took full advantage of this freedom, others still eschewed much of their wealth to conform to the lives of the nuns around them. Elizabeth Woodville, an English queen in the second half of the fifteenth century, spent the last five years of her life at Bermondsey Abbey, and while she never became a nun, the will she made on her deathbed shows that she had almost no worldly possessions to leave to her children.[40] Elizabeth was in good company with countless other European queens who chose the same path for the end of their lives, including Adelaide of Italy, Eleanor of Aquitaine, Hedwig of Silesia, and Joanna of Castile (although the last was forced against her will). Joining the church at the end of her life could have been an ideal way for a medieval woman to find peace.

←← Herrad of Landsberg was a twelfth-century abbess at the monastery of Hohenbourg in Germany. She composed an instruction manual for her fellow nuns, called the *Hortus deliciarum* (Garden of delights), with over 630 pictures, which she may not have illustrated alone. This fantastic page shows Herrad standing with a piece of text alongside portraits of her fellow nuns, an invaluable personal insight into a medieval convent. Sadly, her original manuscript from 1159–75 was destroyed by fire in 1870, though later copies exist.

Herrad of Landsberg and Christian Moritz Engelhardt, *Hortus deliciarum* (Stuttgart and Tübingen, Germany: J. G. Cotta), p. 12, 1818
Bibliothèque Nationale et Universitaire de Strasbourg, France

↙ Tomb effigies of medieval nuns are rare, as they could be seen as contrary to their vows of poverty and the renunciation of worldly goods. However, there were sometimes exceptions for royal nuns or nuns who led their own convents. This is the tomb of prioress Francisquina de Eril, who led the Royal Monastery of Santa María de Sigena in Spain in the late fifteenth century. She is depicted in her nun's habit, eyes closed as if asleep, with her rosary around her neck.

Miguel Ximénez (active c. 1466–1505)
Sepulchral casket of Francisquina de Eril (detail), 1494
Royal Monastery of Santa María de Sigena, Villanueva de Sigena, Huesca, Spain

↑ As time went on, women found that they could live a holy life outside of official orders of nuns. This embroidered panel shows Saint Verdiana Attavanti (*bottom right*), patron saint of Castelfiorentino in Tuscany, who lived from 1192 to 1242 and was renowned for her modesty and holiness. She spent the last thirty-four years of her life in seclusion in a small cell attached to an oratory, though it does not appear that she ever formally joined a religious order.

Scene from the legend of Saint Verdiana Attavanti, Italy (Florence), 1425–50 Linen panel embroidered with silk and metallic threads, 12½ × 18 in. (31.8 × 45.8 cm) Victoria and Albert Museum, London

→→ Saint Hedwig of Silesia was a noblewoman who founded a convent of nuns and retired there after her husband's death, though she never took formal vows. She was revered during her life for her extreme piety, and these scenes show her death and burial, as she is surrounded by nuns praying for her soul. The imagery comes from the *Life of Saint Hedwig* and helped to perpetuate her legacy.

Life of Saint Hedwig, fol. 87r, Poland (Silesia), 1353 Getty, Los Angeles; Ms. Ludwig XI 7

Christianity offered many opportunities for women in medieval Europe. Though the church hierarchy centered around powerful men—bishops, cardinals, and the pope—women were welcomed with open arms to dedicate themselves to God. In a time when women's sexuality and sin were something to be wary of, a woman who wanted to remain a holy virgin of Christ was admirable. By joining the church, a woman took on one of the greatest responsibilities available to her sex at the time. The fate of the world's souls lay on her shoulders, and through her powerful prayers and dedication to religious rules, she could make a real difference. If she experienced visions, then she had a chance to express a knowledge and authority over theological matters that otherwise would have been forbidden. Being a nun was a means for a woman to be heard and respected in her own right, not because of the men she was attached to.

The life of a nun could be difficult, with poverty at the forefront and days spent in isolation, silence, and prayer. But her connection to the outside world was never quite severed, and joining the church could provide a lifestyle more aligned with her personal desires. If a woman did not wish to marry or have children, joining a nunnery could be an appealing prospect. As the Middle Ages developed, there were increasing choices for how women could live a religious life. Whether they wanted the conventional sisterhood of a convent, the solitude of life as an anchoress, the freedom of a beguine, or the glory of a mystic, women found they had far more autonomy to shape their experience as the medieval period progressed.

ne sepelitur b̄ta hedwigis et candor apparuit et odor fragrabat de corpore eius suauissimus

III.   NOBLEWOMEN AND ROYALS

When we look at books written about women in the medieval period, the subjects are very often nobles or royals. The reasons for this are generally twofold: people like to hear about the powerful women who broke the submissive mold that society forced them into at the time, and because sources about high-status women survive in far greater numbers than those of their lower-status counterparts.

These women often had to navigate a complicated web of medieval society that could hold conflicting expectations of them. Noblewomen needed to be the epitome of grace, to be able to charm their husbands, their peers, their courtiers, and even their enemies. They were to be meek and subservient but also fiercely loyal and protective of their children. They had to be able to make interesting conversation, sew, play instruments, and dance with excellence. They should ride and hunt, and also be pious and charitable.

While much of women's education focused on feminine qualities meant to aid them at court, there was also the expectation that they would marry and make powerful political alliances, so they had to be more than pretty ornaments. They would, at some point, have to manage their husband's lands when he was away at war or at court, and they could even become landowners in their own right. They would also have to engage in diplomacy, administer justice, and be the confidantes of queens—or even become queens and rulers themselves. For this they needed social skills and education, to read and write in multiple languages, and to learn the laws of their land and the culture of neighboring territories. They had to be taught well.

EXPECTATIONS OF A NOBLE

Luckily, there were plenty of people on hand to help a noblewoman navigate growing up. Special tutors were often brought in, or the girls were sent to the households of relatives or to court to learn from older women exactly how to behave. There even emerged a new brand of literature aimed at guiding young women. One very popular example was written in the early 1370s and became known as *The Book of the Knight of La Tour Landry*, in reference to its writer, a knight from Anjou named Geoffroy. A widower, Geoffroy had already written an instruction manual for his sons and decided his daughters needed guidance as they were without a mother to learn from.

Geoffroy's manual covers all the different aspects of expected behavior for good women and gives plenty of examples of those who

Fra Filippo Lippi (c. 1406–1469)
Portrait of a Woman with a Man at a Casement, Italy, c. 1440
Detail of page 111

99

↑ A mirror frame with the bust of a beautiful woman looking serene and demure provides a reminder of how women were supposed to present themselves.

Mirror frame, Italy (Siena), 1475–1500
Painted and gilded papier-mâché,
18 × 16⅜ in. (45.7 × 41.6 cm)
Victoria and Albert Museum, London

↗ A group of courtiers takes a stroll in the woods in this fifteenth-century carving. Small mirrors would have been carried around, and so they were often beautifully decorated to reflect the tastes and status of their owners. They were also popular gift choices—the artwork could represent a message between the bestower of the gift and the receiver.

Cover of a mirror case, southern Netherlands, c. 1425
Ivory, diameter: c. 4⅛ in. (10.5 cm)
Rijksmuseum, Amsterdam

↗↗ Geoffroy de la Tour Landry, a French knight, wrote an instruction manual for his daughters to teach them how to grow up into respectable ladies. This copy of the manuscript shows Geoffroy lecturing his three daughters, who are wearing fashionable headdresses and standing demurely.

Geoffroy IV de la Tour Landry, *The Book of the Knight of La Tour Landry*, fol. 1r, France, 15th century
Bibliothèque Municipale, Châteauroux, France; Ms 004

ignored these rules—and suffered as a result. His daughters needed to be holy, not desire earthly riches, be meek and "easy in speech, and in answer courteous and gentle." They should not contradict men but be obedient to their husbands. They were not to paint their faces or pluck their brows to make themselves "the fairer to the pleasing of the world."[1] For the women in his book, failing to follow any of these guidelines often led to death and torture in hell or, at the very least, losing the love of their husbands.

Christine de Pisan, who was born just a few years before Geoffroy penned his book, went on to became a renowned writer and make a living from scripting such types of advice. Her father served the king of France, and so Christine was well positioned to learn from the noblewomen at court. One of her most famous pieces was *The Treasure of the City of Ladies*, which she presented to the king's daughter-in-law, Margaret of Burgundy. Pisan's aim in the book was to advise women of all levels in life, from prostitutes to nuns. She too maintains that women should be demure and modest, with courteous manners, for "a lady is more feared and respected and held in greater reverence when she is seen to be wise and chaste."[2]

As the Middle Ages progressed and women became more and more visible in public life, an increasing number of written tracts emerged that defended and exalted women. One of the most influential was *De claris mulieribus* (*Concerning Famous Women*), written by Florentine author Giovanni Boccaccio in the early 1360s. Boccaccio's book was a compilation of biographies of various women from the Bible, ancient mythology, history, legend, and contemporary times.

In all, he recorded the lives of over one hundred women, and the book was incredibly popular, remaining in print into the Renaissance. Manuscripts of Boccaccio's work often illustrated the women discussed, and as a result they are invaluable sources for learning how women were portrayed in the medieval period. The women were usually shown in medieval dress, rather than ancient outfits of their time, and this added a sense that anything these women were portrayed doing was something medieval women could do too. The art subtly changes the narrative from a story recounting something women of the past did into a template and model for "modern" women.

Such writings were intended to simultaneously justify the contributions of women in society and encourage those in positions of power to live up to the stellar reputations of those who went before them. In 1483, Italian humanist Giovanni Sabadino degli Arienti wrote his own series of biographies of famous women who used their feminine talents to lead them to success. He sent a copy to Isabella d'Este, the nine-year-old daughter of the Duke of Ferrara, who wrote to him that she would "read it attentively, and we will attempt to follow in the footsteps of those illustrious ladies."[3] Later in life, Isabella became Marchioness of Mantua and was considered

↑ Although women were betrothed at a young age and underwent a serious education to prepare for their future role, that does not mean they lacked normal childhoods. They would play with dolls like this one, in the form of a girl, a style popular in southern Germany in the late Middle Ages; she wears a distinctive headdress known as a *Kruseler*.

Kruseler doll, Germany, c. 1350
Spielzeugmuseum Nürnberg, Germany

one of the leading women of the Italian Renaissance, so it appears she took Giovanni's teachings to heart.

Noble and royal women had to constantly think of their behavior in society, as they and their families would be judged on how well they succeeded. Women who could balance the conflicting expectations placed upon them were revered after their death: Philippa of Hainault, queen of England from 1328 to 1369, was remembered in such terms—one chronicler exclaimed that, "as long as she lived, the kingdom of England had grace, prosperity, honor and all good fortune." But those who were seen as overstepping feminine boundaries could find their reputation ripped to shreds. Another English queen, Margaret of Anjou, encountered this the following century when she tried to keep the kingdom going during the mental-health crises of her husband, Henry VI. Though some admired Margaret's strength and determination, her assertiveness, and the building civil war, led to many rumors about her—including claims that her only son was the result of an adulterous affair, and that the king's mental state was a result of her poisoning him.[4]

Nobles and royals lived luxuriously while having many responsibilities, meaning that even times of relaxation could be opportunities for fulfilling one's duty. Though women could rule in their own right and had authority to give orders to their servants and tenants, their power mostly tended to be soft. Noble and royal women were expected to use their social influence to achieve their individual aims and especially those of their families. They were to write letters, host dinners, and use their social connections to get things done. Life at a medieval court provided plenty of opportunities for such action, and this meant that learning how to succeed in leisurely activities could lead to success elsewhere.

Noblewomen learned how to dance for balls, to play chess and skittles, and to hunt. These pastimes were ubiquitous in the art that decorated the world around them, from the tapestries that warmed the walls of their many homes to the mirror cases they carried in their pockets. Women are always at the heart of these depictions, showing that they were seen as central to these leisure activities—which were not just fun for the men of the world. Hunting was one of the most popular sports among the nobility of Europe, with untamed wilds and stocked parks all coming under the control of the wealthy and powerful. Special hunting lodges akin to small palaces were constructed to host groups of nobles, and great feasting upon the spoils usually followed. Women would give chase on horseback, use their personal hawks and hounds to pursue their prey, and shoot at herded game with their bows at "trysts," special stands erected for this type of hunt.[5] They would hunt with their husbands, with large royal parties, or privately with their female friends. Hunting was a perfect intersection between a pastime done for pleasure and one done for business, where noblewomen could renew their social and political ties while relaxing from their usual duties.

The game of chess also sat at the juncture between play and reputation in the Middle Ages. While it was indeed intended for fun, throughout the medieval period the mental exercise of chess

← ← Noblewomen were expected to show a level of piety and religious devotion. This drawing of Margaret of York, Duchess of Burgundy, at prayer with her ladies-in-waiting, is found in a manuscript of moral and religious treatises made as a gift to her. By depicting Margaret in this context, the artist was complementing the lessons in the book and reminding the duchess of her expected duties and behavior.

David Aubert (active 1458–1479)
Moral and religious treatises, fol. 115r, Flanders (Ghent), 1475
Bodleian Libraries, University of Oxford, England; MS. Douce 365

↙ ↙ Christine de Pisan wrote for noble and royal patrons, including the queen of France, Isabeau of Bavaria. This image from one of her manuscripts depicts Christine presenting the book to the queen, giving us a rare insight not only into the mind of a female author but also into the clothes and design of chambers at the time. Royals and nobles would hold court in their bedchambers, and it was not unusual for Isabeau to receive a guest like Christine in hers. Christine carefully supervised the decoration of this manuscript by various artists.

Master of the Cité des Dames (active c. 1400–1415); Master of the Duke of Bedford (active c. 1405–1465)
Christine de Pisan, *Book of the Queen*, fol. 3r, France, c. 1414
British Library, London; Harley MS 4431

also became respected for its use in training tactical skills. All good knights were expected to learn chess just as they were expected to learn how to ride a horse. But as chess became more closely tied to chivalric culture, it also took on a common trope in medieval romances. The back-and-forth of a game of chess was an apt metaphor for the games of love that were played out at court and in literature, and the story of a chess match between a man and woman became a regular trope. A famous example is the Catalan poem *Scachs d'amor*, written around 1475 by a group of Aragonese nobles and poets. The poem describes a match between Mars, Venus, and Mercury and is believed to be the earliest recorded game of chess under modern rules, but in addition to describing a full match of chess, the poem acts as an allegory for love.[6] Games of chess were common motifs in medieval art, and they were depicted in manuscripts and on everyday items used by women, such as mirror cases.

Though men were the strong knights going out to war, noblewomen also played a key role in chivalric culture. They were expected to inspire knights to perform great deeds; ladies would sit in the stands of tournaments and jousts, bestowing their favors upon worthy knights who would compete for their affection. A noblewoman had to play the part to be worthy of a knight, and knowing the skills and language of the court was a key part in this.

One of the most important duties of noble or royal women was to show grace through intercession. Women were expected to be gentle and merciful and, through their more emotional nature, appeal to the harsher side of their husbands. Medieval Europe could be a cruel place, and capital punishment went hand in hand with physical maiming and other severe punishments. This was seen as necessary to maintain law and order, but people still recognized that there were times for clemency. A male ruler, though, risked appearing weak and having his power undermined if he granted it. His wife could therefore play a key role. She could appeal to her husband and ask for mercy in a particular case, and he would grant her this plea as a sign of his affection for her and not through weakness of his character.[7] In this way, a charade was played out that allowed the best outcome for all involved. The man was diplomatic without losing his credibility, the criminal gained a pardon, and the woman bolstered her reputation as a moderating influence.

Sometimes women could partake in dramatic, public displays of intercession. Joan of Navarre, Duchess of Brittany, did so in 1391, when she burst into her husband's chambers in her nightdress, while heavily pregnant and carrying two of her children, to beg him to reconsider arresting a group of French ambassadors.[8] Most of the time, though, the act of intercession was much more official and regulated. Several times a year, a woman would pass on a request to her husband, who in turn would grant her wishes. Importantly, this was not an outright challenge to the authority of her husband but merely a requested change to his judgment, which he would consider and approve. Sometimes these requests were channeled to a husband as and when the woman deemed it necessary, but in many regions, certain events like a queen's coronation or childbirth

This casket is covered in delicately carved scenes of romances that would have been familiar to nobles across Europe. Women are woven throughout—watching knights joust, defending the Castle of Love, and in scenes from various legends and stories. The casket is thought to have been a courtship gift because of its romantic themes.

Casket with scenes of romances, France (Paris), 1330–50
Ivory with modern iron mounts, 4⅝ × 9⅞ × 5 in. (11.8 × 25.2 × 12.9 cm)
Walters Art Museum, Baltimore

were seen as particular occasions when a woman was expected to perform an act of intercession. In these cases, it was expected that her husband would accept the requests. These events were orchestrated to find causes that matched the proceedings or were seen as particularly worthy. Intercessions could range from pardoning prisoners to bestowing a gift or favor upon a loyal servant.

MARRIAGE AND CHILDBIRTH

Unless they became nuns, women in medieval Europe were expected at some point in life to marry and, ideally, have children. As we've seen, there was a much stronger cultural pressure in the south of Europe, where women tended to marry younger, but for all nobles and royals, this duty was anticipated from birth. Lower-class women were usually free to marry later in their twenties and

←← Noblewomen went hunting as a leisure sport but also as a way to build social ties they might need for diplomacy. In this scene, which once decorated a casket, two women use falcons to hunt on horseback alongside men. Caskets could be used to store a variety of objects, from saintly relics to jewelry or clothes. It is unclear what this casket would have been used for, but it was far larger than most surviving caskets from the Middle Ages and must have been expensive.

Panel with hunting scenes, France, c. 1350
Ivory, 4¼ × 12⅛ × ⅛ in. (11 × 30.8 × 0.5 cm)
Metropolitan Museum of Art, Cloisters, New York

↙↙ Women from myth and legend were often depicted in medieval art in a contemporary setting. In this scene, the ancient Roman goddess Diana the Huntress is shown hunting deer with a group of ladies in medieval outfits, with a medieval castle in the distance—a scene that would have been familiar to noblewomen.

Robinet Testard (active c. 1471–1531)
Evrart de Conty, *Le Livre des échecs amoureux moralisés*, fol. 116r, France, 1496–98
Bibliothèque Nationale de France, Paris; Français 143

→ Every chivalric knight was expected to be skillful at chess, but noblewomen were also expected to learn how to play well. Men and women playing each other at chess became a symbol of the game of courtly love and was commonly depicted, as on this ivory mirror case.

A Game of Chess, Paris, c. 1300
Ivory, 4⅛ × 4⅛ × ⅝ in.
(10.4 × 10.5 × 1.7 cm)
Victoria and Albert Museum, London

↘ Noblewomen were expected to inspire knights to great deeds under the name of love and chivalry. This miniature shows a beautiful lady giving a decorated pageant helmet to a kneeling knight so that he can take part in a tournament.

Jehan de Grise (active 1325–1345)
The Romance of Alexander (detail), fol. 101v, Flanders (Tournai), 1338–44
Bodleian Libraries, University of Oxford, England; MS. Bodl. 264

→→ Although women did not partake in jousts and tournaments, they still had important roles not only as spectators but as sponsors. In addition to rousing participants, they would reward victors of competitions. Depictions of such events in art always show women watching excitedly.

Codex Manesse, fol. 52r, Switzerland, 1300–1340
Heidelberg University Library, Germany, Cod. Pal. germ. 848

choose their husbands, but nobles and royals were far likelier to have their spouse chosen for them at a young age. While it still was uncommon for noblewomen to be married before the canonical age of consent—when they reached their teens—their parents did not shy away from betrothing them at a much younger age. Sometimes, these deals were made even before a woman was born. In 1464, Lord William Hastings, an English baron, undertook an agreement with future queen Elizabeth Woodville that her oldest son would marry one of his as yet unborn daughters or nieces, were one to be born within the next six years.[9]

Some noblewomen, and even royals, however, managed to marry

for love. This could have been because their political marriages
had not turned out as planned, and they were thus free to choose
a suitable husband of their own, but most of the time a woman
would have such a choice only after she was widowed. European
nobles wanted sons, to whom they could pass their inheritance, but
daughters were no less valued for the alliances that could be made
through marriage. While peasants would marry within their social
sphere, within their own villages and towns, the net of suitable

noble marriages was far flung, and a woman could expect to travel across the country or even abroad to marry her intended. If she was betrothed at a young age, a girl often would be sent to the home of her future husband and his family so that she could be suitably molded to their needs and, if it was in another territory, learn the language and culture of her new home.

Preparing for a marriage was a significant affair for medieval nobles. The reputation of the whole family rested on the splendor of the event, and no daughter could be sent to her new home unprepared. Marriage chests became popular items to be placed in the bride's new quarters, and they would be decorated with beautiful imagery and filled with exquisite clothing and jewels to emphasize her status and power. Women were not treated as disposable pawns, and both their natal family and their grooms were anxious to care for them. This was exemplified in dowries and dowers, which were agreed upon prior to any noble marriage.

A dowry was a gift given by the woman's family to her husband upon her marriage. It consisted of money, presents, and land, as necessary. Since men were the main inheritors of property in large parts of Europe, giving a daughter a dowry was a way to allow her to access a share of her family's wealth. Dowry land often became female-associated and almost separate from the rest of a family's land—a woman's dowry lands would be passed on to her daughter as her own dowry when she got married, and so on.[10] It was not always solely the responsibility of a woman's parents to provide for her dowry, and in countries like Italy, where marriage was a much more significant part of the culture, it was common for extended family members to leave gifts to unmarried female relations as dowry contributions. Wealthy nobles, both men and women, would bestow dowries on favored servants and children of friends, and they would even leave charitable gifts to their parish to pay for the dowries of peasant women who could not afford their own.[11]

This portrait of Dutch noblewoman Lysbeth van Duvenvoorde was painted in the year of her marriage and would have been displayed proudly in the family home. The romance of an ideal medieval marriage is revealed by the text Lysbeth holds, which reads, "Long have I yearned for the man who would open his heart"—even though women of Lysbeth's class were usually expected to marry for politics rather than love.

Portrait of Lysbeth van Duvenvoorde,
Cologne, c. 1430
Oil on parchment, 12⅝ × 7¾ in.
(32 × 20 cm)
Rijksmuseum, Amsterdam

This stunning manuscript image of Elizabeth Woodville, queen of England, was created during her lifetime and is full of symbolism. Elizabeth was not a typical royal bride, as she was a widow with children rather than a virginal young woman. This illustration thus associates her with the Virgin Mary to highlight her virtue and suitability for queenship. She wears red and blue, colors the Virgin was traditionally depicted wearing. She is also surrounded by red and white roses and gillyflowers, which were associated with the Virgin and connected to her personally: the white rose was a symbol of her husband, Edward IV, and the gillyflower was her own symbol.

Skinners' Company Book of the Fraternity of the Assumption of Our Lady (detail), fol. 32v, England (London), 1472
Private collection

These dowries were not intended to be a way to "sell" women, but in many cases a portion was expected to go toward supporting the woman in the future. A counter-gift was also expected in the form of a dower, which a husband would give to his wife to support her, and for nobles this meant pieces of land that would provide long-term security. These were not one-off cash gifts but provided a way for a wife to independently sustain herself in her marriage. Although many European countries upheld systems in which a woman's possessions became the property of her husband during their marriage, dower lands empowered a noblewoman to have her own responsibilities; manage her own farms, manors, and castles; administer her servants; and gain an income through the produce of her land. She could then use this income to pay for her servants, buy her own clothes and jewels, and otherwise care for herself without having to rely on payments from her husband.

Dower lands also served as a woman's inheritance should her husband predecease her, as she retained full control of these lands

During the Middle Ages it was remarkably easy to get married—all you needed was two people to agree to marriage and consummate, which led to many a man seducing a woman with empty promises only to find the marriage enforced by the church. For nobles, though, it was important that marriages were undertaken with witnesses to seal alliances. This decorated initial shows a couple being joined in marriage by a priest with two witnesses.

Vidal de Canellas, *Vidal Mayor*, fol. 197v, northeastern Spain, c. 1290–1310
Getty, Los Angeles; Ms. Ludwig XIV 6

upon his death, as well as anything else he may have left her. Nobles were not marrying off their daughters without providing for any eventuality. The amount of a woman's dower was directly proportional to her status, and it was a key part of a marriage negotiation. No one wanted to be insulted by a poor dower offer, and diplomatic relations could be at risk if a woman was not seen to have received her appropriate resources and swiftly.

Once married, a woman was expected to quickly begin providing heirs for her husband. Becoming a mother was a way for noblewomen to increase their status, for their position as wife had become secure, and they were now able to wield power through their children. Depending on their position within the nobility, their responsibility as parents varied. Those lower down the social ladder often looked after their children until the ages of around seven to ten years, when their sons would be sent to the household of a noble to learn how to be a knight, and their daughters would be sent to the household of their betrothed to get to know the family and learn how to be a good wife. But among royals, children—particularly sons—were given their own independent households. This meant that the children had their own servants, their own homes, and even their own incomes, even from toddler age.[12] Obviously, they were unable to administer these households until they were much older, and while the fathers had ultimate oversight of who was appointed to these households, mothers tended to have the more significant input. They could send their

↑ Noble and royal women often married younger than their lower-ranking counterparts, and their grooms could be significantly older. This picture shows the marriage of Isabella of Valois, just shy of her seventh birthday, and Richard II of England, who was twenty-nine.

Master of the London Wavrin (active c. 1470–1485)
Jean Froissart, *Chronicles*, fol. 268v, Netherlands (Bruges), c. 1480–94
British Library, London;
Royal MS 14 D VI

↗ Lives were written about saints to spread the word of their holiness and good deeds. This painting shows scenes from the life of Saint Elizabeth of Hungary: her betrothal as a baby (*left*) and her later departure to get married, bringing copious treasure with her (*right*). While many medieval women did not marry until they reached their twenties, noble and royal women were often betrothed at young ages for political alliances.

Four Scenes from the Legend of Saint Elizabeth of Hungary (detail), northern Netherlands, c. 1500
Oil on panel, 32⅝ × 61 in. (83 × 61 cm)
Rijksmuseum, Amsterdam

own trusted servants to look after their children, and they might manage their schedules, the clothes bought for them, and the tutors assigned to them.

Childbirth itself became an incredibly ritualized process during the Middle Ages for noble and royal women, and it was a chance for the woman to be the center of attention. Depictions of childbirth are most commonly found in manuscripts, usually accompanying stories of it from history. For something so vital to society, and yet so treacherous for women and so mystical to men, this is no surprise.

With servants available to tend to a woman's work while she was indisposed, noblewomen were able to withdraw from society for a month before their baby was due. They would undertake this confinement in comfortable quarters in one of their manor houses, castles, or palaces. The rooms would be draped in lavish furnishings and kept warm, and the mother-to-be would be attended only by women. Her mother and other female relatives could join alongside her ladies-in-waiting and, when the time came, midwives. This was an intimate moment in a woman's life, and she had the support and wisdom of the women around her, including those who had experienced childbirth and could provide her with particular comfort and care.

The confinement continued after the birth of the child as a way to give the woman a chance to properly recover from the ordeal. Even

←← Although romances were popular courtly literature, the reality for many women of a higher status was that they would be marrying for money and political reasons. It was not unusual for a young woman to marry a much older man, and this dynamic was sometimes satirized in medieval art, as in this drawing where the young woman holds her hand out expectantly for money from the man reaching into his purse.

Albrecht Dürer (1471–1528)
The Ill-Assorted Couple, Germany (Nuremberg), 1493–97
Engraving on paper, 5⅞ × 5⅜ in. (15 × 13.8 cm)
Rijksmuseum, Amsterdam

↑ Noblewomen may have had to travel far from home when they got married, even to new countries and kingdoms. This image shows the grand procession accompanying a noble bride to her new home. She rides on a horse while her ladies follow in a carriage, surrounded by noblemen.

David Aubert (active 1458–1479);
Loyset Liédet (c. 1420–1479)
History of Charles Martel, fol. 78r, southern Netherlands (Bruges, Brussels), 1465
Royal Library of Belgium, Brussels; MS. 7

for the nobility, childbirth was dangerous, and it was common for women and babies to become unwell or die. Violant of Bar, queen of Aragon, wrote poignantly in her letters of her frustration and sorrow at giving birth to children who did not live long; only one of her eleven children survived to adulthood, and several died within a year of being born.[13]

If a woman survived giving birth, then she had a significant celebration to look forward to in her churching ceremony. This tended to be held around a month to forty days later, and it was a way to introduce the woman back into society. In a form of ritual cleansing, she would be accompanied to a celebratory Mass where she would pray, give an offering, and be blessed. After the ceremony, huge feasting and celebrations would occur—for royals, churching celebrations could last for days. Jousting would be held, copious amounts of food and drink consumed, and nobles from across the realm and beyond would be invited to celebrate in this blessing.[14] The woman was at the center, clothed in stunning outfits of the most luxurious material, which were changed often to reflect the wealth and power of the blessed couple.

Being a mother could come with other avenues for power if her husband died when their children were minors. If the woman had been married to a ruler, then one of her children would succeed her husband upon his death. Child rulers variably cropped up across Europe in the Middle Ages, and conflicts could surround their accession if there were adult men who also had claims to the territory. But if a child managed to hold on to their claim, then they needed someone to rule on their behalf until they came of age—a regent. Many

places elected a regency council made up of trusted male relatives and courtiers, but the child's mother very often found a seat at the table.

The mother, as the child's guardian and caregiver and as the wife of the deceased ruler, was a natural candidate for having a say in affairs. In some regions, it was even preferred that the mother become the lead regent of the government. France, which introduced Salic law to prevent the crown going to, or through, a woman, was surprisingly keen on having its queens act as regent—such as the seventh-century Queen Nanthild—yet the English across the water never officially had a queen regent.[15] Many regions were used to wives acting as regent when their husbands were absent during times of war or when they were otherwise away from court, and this made it easier to accept a woman's authority when he died; medieval Aragon, for example, had seven different queens consort (women who were the wives of kings, rather than queens in their own right) who ruled with de jure and de facto authority.[16] Even during a man's lifetime, his wife may have been seen as the better ruler, as was the case with the Duke of Ferrara in late fifteenth-century Italy. It was noted that while the duke "devoted himself to having a good time and playing [cards] and riding around the park," his wife, Eleanor, "listened to the people, heard their pleas, and was accepted by the Ferrarese people."[17] Because mothers were expected to care for and protect the interests of their children above all else, they were theoretically excellent caretakers of the realm until their child heir came of age, as everything they would do was only in the interest of the child and thus the people.

Through marriage and motherhood, noblewomen obtained power

→ The birth of a child was a female-only affair, with the pregnant woman sequestered away where possible. Here, Catherine of Valois, queen of England, rests in bed after giving birth to the future Henry VI. On the right side of the drawing, one of her ladies goes to the door to give the news of the birth to a male messenger.

Caxton Master (active 1470–1490)
The Pageants of Richard Beauchamp, Earl of Warwick (detail), fol. 22v, southern Netherlands (Bruges?), c. 1483
British Library, London; Cotton Julius E. IV, art. 6

→→ Some European territories had a tradition of women acting as regents for their underage sons. This manuscript image shows a scene from France's past, when Queen Nanthild acted as regent for her son, Clovis II. She is seen gently guiding her son with a motherly hand on his arm, reminding viewers that women who acted as regents were supposed to be selfless and to act only in their child's best interests.

Robinet Testard (active c. 1471–1531)
Great Chronicles of France, fol. 66v, France, 1471
Bibliothèque Nationale de France, Paris; Français 2609

that they could not access simply as daughters of the nobility. Their high-ranking blood gave them an opportunity to wield influence and authority over both men and women, as well as the educational opportunities to do so successfully. But a noblewoman could not do this as a maiden, and she had to marry first to access and gain control of land and inheritance. If she were to become widowed, it became acceptable for her to operate as a single woman, or *femme sole*, but first she had to pass the rite of passage of marriage. Her hand was too valuable to her family for her not to.

RUNNING A HOUSEHOLD

Whether a noblewoman was a wife, widow, consort, or ruler, one of her most important duties was to run a household. Women were frequently depicted in a domestic sphere in artwork, tending to children and chores, but for nobles, it was not all homemaking; from the knightly classes up to the monarchy, women of the nobility had incredible responsibility placed on them. Lesser knights would have only a few domestic servants to help cook, clean, garden, and care for horses, but the highest nobles could have vast numbers of people under their command.

The matriarch of the noble household had to ensure her servants were all doing their jobs properly. Her family's properties had to be kept in excellent condition in case any important guests decided to stop by and to ensure that they were suitably reflecting the power and glory of her dynasty. Monarchy in the medieval period was peripatetic, meaning rulers and their families were unlikely to stay in one home for very long as they traveled around the kingdom to see their subjects, reminding them who was in charge. Kings and queens had many palaces and manors of their own, but they might stay with their noble subjects as a sign of favor and a way to build relationships. Pantries needed to be stocked with food, supplies of firewood needed to be built for the winter, and houses needed to be decorated with the most luxurious items as befitting their status, and women oversaw a lot of this work. Beautiful paintings, intricately woven tapestries that spanned entire rooms, and painstakingly sewn soft furnishings were all examples of art and function

overlapping—they kept castles warm, made furniture comfortable, and portrayed the wealth and splendor of one's dynasty while also entertaining and pleasing one's eye. Women were at the heart of this artwork, both creating and commissioning it so that it suited their exact tastes.

Even when household decisions were jointly made between husband and wife, the wife was still often the one giving the instructions. In 1376, the Catalan Aragonese infanta Mata d'Armagnac wrote to one of her officials to explain the payments that she and her husband had decided to give to their servants, and gave specific instructions on how the money should be distributed.[18] Though the couple had decided on this important aspect of their household together, it was Mata and her officials who were in charge of seeing it through.

Women at the highest echelons of society—the duchesses, countesses, and queens—very often had subhouseholds of their own. They had their own servants, they had damsels and ladies-in-waiting attending to them and being their friends and confidantes, and they may even have their own treasury. Administration of this team around them was normally left for the women to supervise themselves, which meant they managed payment of wages and giving of gifts and favors. As women were expected to oversee the well-being of their household, they also had to manage social relations within their courts. They would arrange marriages between their servants

or become godmother to their ladies' children, and they could be turned to when any disputes arose.

As well as helping to administer their husbands' lands, noblewomen and queens were normally landowners in their own right. It was common practice for high-status women to control their dower lands before widowhood, and this was especially expected of a queen. If her husband died before her, then depending on her whereabouts in Europe, the widow might find herself in control of significant swaths of land. In many countries, it was customary for a widow to receive one-third of her husband's lands and income, but in other territories, the distribution could be more generous. In the Prince-Archbishopric of Salzburg prior to the mid-1200s, the widow was usually granted lifelong use of all or most of her husband's property.[19]

Widowhood could prove very freeing for noblewomen—a chance for them to truly wield power and influence without the restraint of a man, to rule over their own castle quite literally. A widow had to guard this freedom tightly, though, as medieval noblemen were not above abducting widows, marrying them, and taking their wealth. However, not all men appreciated this practice, whether that was because their own potential brides were being swept from under their feet or because they were relatives of such women who disliked seeing them used in this way. As a result, various laws were passed to protect the rights of widows. In 1215, several clauses of England's Magna Carta were dedicated to stopping this from happening, including clause eight: "No widow shall be compelled to marry, so long as she wishes to remain without a husband."[20]

The household was the lifeblood of medieval society. Just as leisure pursuits were a combination of business and pleasure, so too was the home of a noble. Homes of the highest levels of society were the hub of administration—not private places where one could shut out the world. Tenants who worked the lands would go to their local manor to receive their wages; feasts and celebrations on holy days and festivals would take place within the great hall of a castle; and diplomatic negotiations would be held in the parlors of palaces. As the household was very much the woman's sphere, this meant that a noblewoman was at the heart of negotiating these many obligations.

Meals were communal affairs, and neighbors, servants, and strangers would be served in the dining hall of a noble's home. In 1412 and 1413, a minor English gentlewoman named Alice de Bryene of Suffolk served an average of forty-five meals per day at her manor hall, showing just how important this service was to even the lesser nobility. Around the same time, the household of the Duchess of

Burgundy was supplying more than seven hundred liters of wine per year to each person in her household, while toward the end of the fifteenth century, the English court provided food for over two thousand people a day through the Christmas season.[21]

Noblewomen found themselves deeply tied to the land, as throughout the Middle Ages, the wealth of the nobility came from landed holdings. As the period progressed, many families found reasonable wealth through skilled professions and merchant trading, but the upper echelons could reach those heights of money and power only through extensive properties, and this meant owning huge swaths of land. Their property was cared for by their servants and the tenants they rented out to, but the noble couple needed to keep a close eye on their affairs to make sure their land was being used to its full potential. Wasteland, overgrown pieces of land, forests improperly managed, and empty fishponds all meant a loss of earning for the owner. This was no small loss, either; in 1330, the agents of Philippa of Hainault, queen of England, reported to her husband that the queen's dower lands in Wales, which had been valued at a staggering £3,000 (more than the annual income of an earl), were in fact worth just £150 (less than what an average knight might expect to earn) because there was no livestock on them and no other way of making money.[22] Although nobles could entrust stewards to care for their land on their behalf, a diligent noble made sure to personally oversee his or her assets.

From queens down to local knightly ladies, women were involved in this process. Women of all statuses were expected to manage and administer their households, and this extended to the land outside it. Moreover, their husbands and fathers were often away from home, whether they were fighting in a war, serving at court, acting as a diplomat, or because they were traveling throughout their landed holdings. This meant women were often expected to undertake the management by themselves, and during harvest season, in particular, this could mean seeing to minute details. At the end of our period, in 1500, the widowed Doña Beatriz Ponce de León had to organize the olive harvest on her estate of Los Santillanes in Seville since her husband was no longer around to do so. In just over one month, Beatriz signed twelve work contracts, hired several teams of women to harvest the olives, and drew up further contracts to organize the clearing and preparation of uncultivated land to expand her agricultural plantings.[23]

PATRONAGE

Serving food and drink to one's neighbors was just one way that noblewomen were expected to fulfill a social contract and give back to society. The Three Estates (chapter 1) worked in careful balance because each provided for the other: the peasants toiled to provide food and goods, the church cared for the realm's spiritual well-being, and the knights fought to protect the kingdom. But this noble third had a wider obligation, beyond just protecting people with their swords, to better society. They were gifted with great wealth, which they could use for silk and jewels and castles, but they also had a moral obligation to give some of this wealth to the poor. They had to dispense charity, hold dinners for their tenants, and donate to the church. The nobles who wanted to be true chivalric heroes needed to go further than this, though. Reputation and legacy were everything to these families, whose high position in society rested largely on the backs of their ancestors. They needed to prove that they were worthy of the respect and responsibility on their shoulders, and they wanted to be remembered after they were gone. By patronizing educational facilities, artists, writers, and architects, nobles could prove their cultural sophistication and show that they were truly high-class aristocrats.

A noblewoman who had not followed a life in the church could still display significant piety and religious devotion. By building churches or commissioning expensive, beautiful objects of devotion to donate to religious sites, she could help speed her way from purgatory to heaven and simultaneously remind all who beheld her patronage of her power and wealth. Those who founded or heavily supported religious communities could also be creating a contingency plan for their future. As we've seen, many noblewomen retired to the communities they had patronized, either in widowhood, in their final years, or even on their deathbed, becoming nuns or vowesses or simply honored guests.[24]

Through patronage, women could also change the culture around them. As noble and royal women frequently traveled to a new territory upon their marriage, they would bring their natal culture with them. They usually transported some servants from their homeland, which helped with the transition, as being presented with a culture with different traditions and expectations could be jarring for a young woman. It was natural that she therefore wanted to bring familiar comforts with her, and paying for artists, writers, and musicians to create pieces of work that reflected her home culture was a way to do this. In order to gain favor with the female ruler, courtiers in her new home would often pick up on the fashions that she had brought with her, and cultures thus mixed and melded. Eleanor of Castile, who became queen of England in the thirteenth century, famously introduced forks to the English court and created the country's first purpose-built tiled bathroom, both things she was familiar with from her Spanish homeland.[25] Sometimes a woman's patronage was indirect, as her people scrambled to please her. When Maria of Aragon, queen of Castile, expressed anger after reading *Il Corbaccio*, a work by Boccaccio that disparaged women as lustful and wicked, a group of writers swiftly composed a series of works in defense of women.[26]

Architecture was a popular form of patronage for medieval noblewomen. By shaping the built environment around them, these women were leaving a very visible and long-lasting mark. Queens helped to build universities, ensuring that scholars of the next generation would remember their glory. They built churches, castles, and palaces, and the evidence shows that many were intricately involved with the design process and did not simply make an order and leave it in someone's hands. Philippa of Hainault created a stunning hall of mirrors and stained glass windows adjacent to a dancing room at Windsor Castle, while Jeanne of Navarre, queen of France, left detailed instructions in her will for the creation of Paris's first royal college, including its intended architectural layout.[27] Acting as a patron was as much a way for women to express their creativity and individuality as to show their power, piety, or generosity.

FEMALE RULERS

Our perception of the medieval period is that of a time mired in sexism, and so—perhaps influenced by the widespread knowledge of the obsession of Henry VIII to sire a male heir—we expect that

Although many statues in churches were religious in nature, wealthy nobles who donated money and other gifts to churches could also be commemorated on interior and exterior walls. Uta von Ballenstedt, also known as Uta of Naumburg, Margravine of Meissen, was one of twelve people who donated funds to create Naumburg Cathedral. A stonemason was commissioned to honor them for their generous contributions. Statues like Uta's were made not only to thank donors but to encourage others to donate their own wealth and to pray for the donors. Uta's statue was made famous by Walt Disney, who used it as a model for the evil stepmother in *Snow White*.

Uta of Naumburg (detail), Germany, 13th century
Gilded and painted sandstone
Naumburg Cathedral, Germany

Finding images of identifiable medieval women can be difficult, as painted portraits of women only began near the end of the Middle Ages. Images of nobles and royals can, however, often be found in the pages of devotional religious books, and female patrons and donors turn up frequently in books of hours intended for use by women. The original owner of this book is shown kneeling to the right of this depiction of the Pietà (the Virgin Mary cradling the dead body of Jesus) and, interestingly, she is given great prominence as her scale exceeds that of the holy group.

Book of hours (detail), fol. 114r, France (Rouen), c. 1400–90
Walters Art Museum, Baltimore; W.225

Noble and royal women were expected to use their wealth for the common good, and many chose to build churches as a way to show their piety and contribute to the salvation of their souls and those of others. This illustration from a life of Saint Hedwig shows her as High Duchess consort of Poland convincing her husband to provide her with funds to build a convent for nuns in their territory (*top*), and nuns settling at the new convent (*bottom*). Hedwig appears as the driving force behind the project, personally directing and overseeing construction and ushering the nuns in once it is completed.

Life of Saint Hedwig, fol. 56r, Poland (Silesia), 1353
Getty, Los Angeles; Ms. Ludwig XI 7

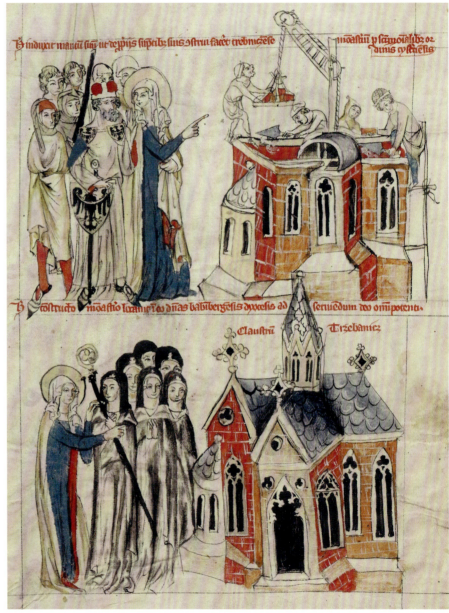

medieval nobles were disappointed to have daughters and that only men could inherit. While some countries did introduce laws to prevent women from inheriting the crown, most prominently France, plenty of European countries did not, theoretically, have a problem with a queen regnant—a ruler in her own right. It was common for nobles to have only female heirs, and it was accepted that these daughters and sisters would inherit the lands and titles of their male relatives without question. Many women therefore ruled important, wealthy, and powerful lands across Europe throughout this period. Their control of these lands was usually respected, and it made them very attractive options on the marriage market.

Such female rulers are found everywhere in medieval art. Rulers of both sexes adorn manuscripts that recount their deeds, particularly chronicles, which were a popular way to record history as it was happening. Portraits of women rulers turn up in charters that they granted and in church books recording their generous donations to institutions. They were able to shape their own iconography by commissioning their own depictions of themselves, such as the portrait all female rulers needed on the seal used for their documents, or a tomb effigy to ensure their memory outlived them. By controlling the creation of these pieces, they could communicate whatever message they wanted.

Women who ruled their own territories were expected to fulfill the same roles as their male counterparts, even if they were often aided by their husbands. They would dispense justice, settle disputes among their subjects, patronize the arts, support religious institutions, and engage in diplomatic relations with their neighbors. These women could spark fierce loyalty from their subjects, particularly when men from other regions tried to interfere with their rule. Their subjects would rather submit to the control of a native woman than risk being pawns in the games of powerful men. Eleanor of Aquitaine, one of the most famous women of twelfth-century Europe, found that her subjects in Aquitaine and Poitou wanted to answer only to her after her marriage to Henry II, as they desired to avoid being swept up under the control of the English king, who might ignore their own customs and laws.[28]

Some smaller territories, such as Hainault in the Low Countries, had long traditions of women inheriting. These areas had long dispelled any misgivings about having a female ruler and so were happy to fight for these women's rights. This was the situation Countess Jacqueline (also known as Jacoba of Bavaria) found herself in during the 1420s and 1430s when she restarted the Hook and Cod wars—civil wars named for the two opposing factions, the Cods apparently taking their name from the fish-scale motif on the coat of arms of their first leader, William of Bavaria, and their enemies becoming became Hooks because a hook is used to catch a cod. Jacqueline had been married as a teenager to a French prince, but he died from a suspected poisoning when she was sixteen, and her father died two months after that. Without the power of the French monarchy to support Jacqueline's claims to her father's territories, her uncle John, the bishop of Liège, claimed them for himself.

Margaret of Navarre, queen of Sicily, corresponded with Thomas Becket, archbishop of Canterbury, during his lifetime, expressing her support for him against the English king, Henry II—who would have Becket killed in 1170. A few years later, when her son married Henry II's daughter, Bishop Reginald of Bath gifted Margaret relics of Saint Thomas Becket encased in this pendant. On the front of the pendant, an engraving depicts Queen Margaret being blessed by the bishop.

Reliquary pendant, England (Canterbury), 1174–77
Gold, 2 × 1¼ × ¼ in. (5 × 3.1 × 0.7 cm)
Metropolitan Museum of Art, New York

Jacqueline was quickly remarried to the Duke of Brabant, but they greatly disliked each other, and the duke was in considerable financial difficulty. Jacqueline fled to the English court for support, where she engaged in a potentially bigamous marriage with an English prince, the Duke of Gloucester, in order to gain new allies in her fight for her lands. Jacqueline had obtained a form of annulment from the antipope Benedict XIII, but his authority was not universally recognized across Europe due to the existence of his rival in the Papal Schism, Pope Martin V. Many people considered Jacqueline and the Duke of Brabant to be married still—including the duke himself—and thus her marriage to Gloucester illegal. Her subjects rallied for her cause, and many in her territories of Holland and Hainault proved happy to die by the sword to defend her right to rule. However, a series of disasters, and her eventual abandonment by the Duke of Gloucester, overwhelmed her, and Jacqueline ultimately had to cede her territories to her cousin, the Duke of Burgundy.[29]

While many women ruled smaller regions with little trouble, it was rarer to find a woman in the position of inheriting a whole kingdom. Duchies and other parcels of lands were still ultimately under the influence of male monarchs of neighboring countries, who were usually their overlords. But a queen regnant answered to no one (apart from, perhaps, the pope) and wielded far more wealth and power than her noble counterparts. Though many people had no problem with the theory of a woman ruling, some queens found that once their reign was put into practice their male subjects could not deal with the reality.

Mary I, the oldest daughter of Henry VIII, is regarded as the first queen regnant of England, rising to the throne in 1553, outside of our period. But centuries before her, another woman came tantalizingly close to holding this title. Empress Matilda was referred to in her time as "Lady of the English," and in the eyes of many, she was the true monarch of the country—but she was never formally crowned or declared queen, and thus the official title goes to Mary. Matilda was born in 1102, one of two legitimate children of Henry I of England. Her brother died in a tragic shipwreck known as the *White Ship* disaster, in which hundreds of young nobles drowned in the channel between England and France.[30] As a result, Matilda became her father's only heir.

Henry I did not despair at having a daughter succeed him, as his later namesake did, and until the end of his life he did everything possible to ensure that Matilda would have a smooth accession. He made his nobles swear allegiance to her, and married her to the heir of the Count of Anjou to give her a powerful ally. Despite all of Henry's work, when he died, Matilda was outside the country, pregnant, and consolidating her military hold in Normandy, and her cousin Stephen, the Count of Boulogne, raced to England from France to have himself declared king instead. Though Stephen was fairly popular at the start of his reign, Matilda had powerful relations on her side. Her uncle was king of Scotland, and he invaded the north of England for Matilda, while her half brother, a powerful

← ← Noble and royal women often had a hand in designing their own tombs and those of their spouses. As the Middle Ages progressed, tomb effigies became more and more personalized, depicting the person true to life rather than idealized. Eleanor of Castile was portrayed in such a way in her joint tomb with her husband, Charles III of Navarre. Eleanor acted as regent during her husband's absence on multiple occasions.

Tomb of Charles III of Navarre and Eleanor of Castile (detail), 1413–19
Pamplona Cathedral, Spain

↙ ↙ Jacqueline of Hainault, also known as Jacoba of Bavaria, became a ruler in her own right, but a series of unsuccessful marriages jeopardized her leadership position and eventually caused her to lose her territories. This portrait of her complemented one of her fourth and final husband, whom she was able to marry for love. The two paintings hung in the couple's home, though this version appears to be a slightly later copy.

Jacoba of Bavaria, Countess of Holland and Zeeland, northern Netherlands, c. 1480s
Oil on panel, 25⅛ × 19⅝ in. (64 × 50 cm)
Rijksmuseum, Amsterdam

English noble, started a rebellion from within the country. England quickly descended into a civil war known as the Anarchy.

Despite being a woman, Matilda was supported by many in England because of her strong claim as the only surviving legitimate child of the previous monarch, and having the allegiance and forces of powerful family members strengthened her position. The Anarchy lasted for fifteen years, which shows the extent of her support, but ultimately the English nobles could not tolerate a woman ruling over them. At one stage, Matilda had captured Stephen and begun preparations for her coronation, but her behavior was seen as haughty and overbearing, and this lost her the support of Londoners, who rose up and expelled her from the city.[31] She never got as close

to the throne again. Matilda had behaved only as a male monarch
would have done in order to defend his right to rule, but in a woman
these actions were considered unnatural and unacceptable.

More than two centuries after Matilda's attempt at the crown,
Poland had its first female monarch. Jadwiga was born in the 1370s,
one of two surviving daughters of King Louis of Hungary and Poland.
The king, like Henry I of England, wanted to ensure his kingdoms
stayed in his family's control after his death, so he worked as hard
as he could to ensure that would happen. He betrothed Jadwiga
and her older sister Mary to powerful European men—William of
Austria and Sigismund of Luxembourg, respectively—so that they
would have the support of strong families and kingdoms behind

them. After King Louis's death, Mary was swiftly crowned king of Hungary, but the Polish were not keen to have her as their ruler.

The subjects of Poland were less concerned about having a female monarch than about having monarchs who consistently favored and lived in Hungary instead of their own lands. The nobles of the country announced they would obey only the daughter of Louis who would settle in Poland, and they started to look around for alternatives to Mary and Jadwiga; it didn't help that both of their fiancés were also unpopular. The girls' mother, Elizabeth, was anxious to ensure that the rights of her daughters were protected, and so she offered to change the succession plans so that Mary was named king of Hungary, and Jadwiga would become king of Poland and reside in that country.

While Elizabeth delayed sending Jadwiga to Poland, the Duke of Masovia tried to steal the throne from under her as Stephen had done to Matilda centuries before. Luckily for Jadwiga, the loyal citizens of Kraków closed the city gates before he arrived. This display convinced the archbishop of Gniezno to refuse to perform the coronation for the duke, giving Elizabeth and Jadwiga time to act. Jadwiga was crowned king of Poland in 1384 and ruled until her death from childbirth complications in 1399. It is thought that Jadwiga and her sister were crowned as kings rather than queens in order to emphasize that they were queens regnant, not consorts, and thus the highest authority in the land. Jadwiga's rule was widely accepted by her Polish subjects and saw an increase in the territories under Poland's control. She was known for her charitable works and the promotion of the vernacular in church services, and became venerated by her subjects shortly after her death.[32] For her people, being a woman made her no less of a king.

Some female rulers were so powerful that they even created geographic entities of their own. Margaret I of Denmark, Norway, Sweden, and Finland was born in 1353 and became a legendary monarch. Margaret was initially a queen consort through her marriage to King Haakon VI of Norway and Sweden, but after the death of both Haakon and their son and heir, Margaret was proclaimed queen of the Scandinavian kingdoms in her own right. Soon after taking power, Margaret decided that her kingdoms should be joined together, and she created the Kalmar Union, to be ruled by a single monarch. Margaret allowed for individual laws and customs of each country to remain, with the vision of them growing closer over time. She held ambitious dreams for her legacy, entering into an alliance with England to be sealed with a double wedding between her great-nephew and heir, Eric, and Princess Philippa of England; and Eric's sister, Catherine, and the English heir, Prince Henry. It was her hope that by joining the heirs of both kingdoms, she could recreate the northern Viking powerhouse of centuries past. Margaret died in 1412, but the Kalmar Union survived in various guises for more than a century after her death.[33]

WOMEN WHO FOUGHT

In most cultures around the world, it was usually men who went to war, while women only provided domestic support or sexual comfort, or suffered as victims. Although this was the case in medieval Europe, noble and royal women were much more involved in warfare than we might expect. These women were often left at home while their husbands were away at court or fighting in the many, many wars that raged across Europe, and sometimes these wars would come to their doorsteps. Whether facing petty squabbles with local rivals or the savage front line of an invading kingdom, noblewomen were not infrequently the ones left to defend their houses, castles, and towns against their enemies. These women had armies of men who would rally to defend them, but some took the responsibility of being a noble to a personal level and picked up the chain of command themselves.

Noblewomen were trained to be efficient and skilled in exerting authority over their inferiors and in organizing people from all parts of society. They were shrewd in politics and knew how to create propaganda and inspire loyalty when needed—skills they could use to command soldiers. An excellent example of a woman who embodied these skills in the face of her enemies was Agnes Randolph, Countess of Dunbar and March. A Scottish noblewoman of the fourteenth century, Agnes found herself in a showdown with the English during the Second War of Scottish Independence. Facing the forces of the Earl of Salisbury, one of the most trusted servants of Edward III of England, many others would have seen defeat as inevitable—but not Agnes.

She rallied her own troops and simultaneously disparaged the enemy by acting as if the English were no threat at all. When their initial catapult shots damaged the ramparts of Dunbar Castle, Agnes had her ladies-in-waiting dust the ramparts with handkerchiefs. When the English then brought her captured brother in front of the castle and threatened to hang him, she shrugged off the threat by exclaiming that it would only benefit her, as she would inherit his lands. After six months of torment, the English were forced to

←← Jadwiga was Poland's first queen regnant, although she was known as King Jadwiga to emphasize her sole authority. Her majesty is shown on her royal seal, where she sits enthroned with a crown and scepter.

Seal of Jadwiga of Poland, 1385
Archiwum Narodowy, Kraków, Poland

↖↖ Noblewomen had their own seals, as they conducted business on their own behalf as well as for their husbands. The imagery on a woman's seal can give us information about how she wanted to be portrayed to the wider world; Helwig von Ysenburg is seen here holding a falcon.

Seal of Helwig von Ysenburg, 1274
Schlossmuseum Braunschweig, Germany

↑ Queen Margaret I of Denmark, Norway, Sweden, and Finland created the Kalmar Union, an ambitious uniting of her kingdoms. She was remembered fondly after her death in 1412, and this grand tomb effigy was created a decade later to properly commemorate a glorious queen.

Johannes Junge (active 1406–after 1428)
Tomb of Margaret I (detail), 1423
Roskilde Domkirke, Denmark

→ Women were sometimes depicted wearing armor, though this was usually in a mythical context, as in this print from a series illustrating an update by Giacomo Filippo Foresti (also known as Fra Jacopo Philippo Bergomensis) of Giovanni Boccaccio's *De claris mulieribus* (*Concerning Famous Women*).

Woman in armor with spear and coat of arms, Italy (Ferrara), 1480–97/99
Print on paper, 2½ × 2¾ in. (6.5 × 7.1 cm)
Rijksmuseum, Amsterdam

→→ Though warrior women were rare in medieval Europe, artists enjoyed depicting women in this role, particularly those from legend or ancient history. This image shows the execution of Cyrus the Great, founder of the Persian Empire and king of the Medes, by Tomyris (or Thamaris), a sixth-century BC queen of the Massagetai of central Asia.

Boucicaut Master (active c. 1390–1430)
Cases of Noble Men and Women, fol. 58r,
France (Paris), 1413–15
Getty, Los Angeles; Ms. 63

admit defeat and abandon their siege of the castle, having lost great amounts of money and time and suffered a blow to their reputation.[34]

Agnes's ferocity in defending her home should have come as no surprise to the English; just over a decade prior, their own queen had taken up the military mantle in a far more extreme capacity. While it was accepted that noblewomen and queens might, if required, lead soldiers to defend their homes, they were not expected to spearhead aggressive troops or raise armies in their own names—though this is exactly what Queen Isabella of France, wife of Edward II of England, had done in the 1320s. Edward II was widely known to show obsessive favoritism to male nobles, and throughout his reign this had raised tensions with the rest of Edward's subjects. The country had teetered on the edge of civil war in the 1310s due to the elevation of one of Edward's favorites, but—having not learned his lesson—he had new favorites at court by the 1320s. Isabella had held a respected position at her husband's court, as was her due, but Edward's favorites were powerful enough to displace her. She found her influence reduced, but the greatest insult came when Edward confiscated swaths of her lands.

Angry and humiliated, Isabella found reason to escape to the court of her brother, the French king Charles IV. After some careful plotting, which saw her obtain control of her son and Edward's heir, the future Edward III, Isabella put her plans into action. Gathering exiled English nobles who had also suffered from coming into conflict with Edward's favorites—and making an (illegal) marriage alliance with her cousin, the Countess of Hainault, for their children, wherein Prince Edward was betrothed to the countess's daughter, Philippa, in return for ships and soldiers—Isabella landed

in England with a small army.[35] Isabella was loved and trusted in England, while Edward II and his actions were loathed, and she swiftly found more and more men pledging their swords to her cause, including Edward's own half brothers. Isabella, with the help of powerful male nobles, successfully captured her husband and his favorites and eventually forced Edward II to abdicate in favor of their son. Of course, being a caring mother, Isabella took up the heavy burden of ruling—and spending England's gold reserves—for several years in her son's place.[36]

Both Agnes and Isabella were able to wield such military power because they played into the cultural norms of their times. Women were supposed to be submissive to men and not worry themselves with matters of war, but there were exceptions when family was involved. Agnes was defending her husband's lands, while Isabella acted as a concerned wife and mother. Isabella had performed a great act of propaganda prior to her invasion, donning widow's clothing and claiming that Edward's favorites had come between husband and wife, a violation of a sacred bond, to such an extent that it was as if she were a widow.[37] Claiming she simply wanted to remove these interlopers to be reunited with her husband, and

simultaneously defend the inheritance of her son, meant that she could portray herself as a responsible noblewoman who was trying to restore natural order, rather than a woman subverting her expected role to take up the sword and remove her husband.

Women military leaders were depicted with surprising frequency in medieval art, particularly as the period progressed. Artwork would often show women from popular stories in myth, legend, and ancient history as warriors, dressed in armor and wielding weapons. But as time went on and there were more contemporary examples of women fighting for a cause—and the writing of chronicles recording present histories proliferated—more and more pictures illustrated the deeds of these women. The artists did not shy away from showing women leading troops and standing in the heart of battle, though they were usually depicted wearing dresses to show their femininity rather than full suits of armor. Occasionally, to demonstrate that they were both capable military leaders and in danger, they might be shown with a breastplate over their dresses, as in the image of Joan of Arc in chapter II. It is interesting that these women are depicted without judgment; there is nothing unnatural about Joan in that picture or about Isabella in the manuscript illustration on the facing page. Though these leaders stand out by virtue of their sex and their clothing, the artists did not demonize the women or show them behaving improperly. In fact, these women are seen as inspirational figures, commanding troops and rousing them with their words and presence. Such images reveal contemporary attitudes toward noblewomen and queens who assumed military roles.

While the majority of noblewomen who took up arms did so in defense of their families, homes, or kingdoms, for just a short period of time, one woman turned to a life of violence out of vengeance. Jeanne de Clisson was a French noblewoman, born in 1300, who lived in Brittany. Jeanne married four times (not unusual for a woman in her position), but it was the life, or more accurately the death, of her third husband that would define her life. This man was Olivier IV de Clisson, a wealthy Breton noble who controlled significant areas of land. The couple got caught up in the Breton War of Succession, fought to decide who should be the next ruler of Brittany—which was actually a thinly veiled excuse for the French and English to reignite their wars against each other, each backing a different candidate.

During this war, Olivier was defending the city of Vannes from the English, when the city eventually fell, and he was captured. Of all the important prisoners taken by the English, Olivier was the only one released in exchange for a captured English noble and a small sum of money. The low ransom requested for Olivier created mistrust among the French, who suspected he may have been in league with the English. After peace was made between England and France in 1343, Olivier was invited to a tournament by the French and arrested upon his arrival. He was put on trial for treason, and despite Jeanne's best efforts to save him, he was executed as a common criminal, his body desecrated and put on display. His gruesome treatment shocked the French nobles and was greatly criticized, but

Isabella of France, queen of England, broke female norms when she launched an invasion against her husband, Edward II. By portraying herself as an aggrieved widow who had been forcibly separated from her husband and as a mother protecting the rights of her son, she was able to gain significant support for her conquest. In these images depicting Isabella's invasion (*bottom row*), she is shown at the heart of the siege of Bristol, which she personally led. Her attack was successful—she rescued her two daughters and captured her husband's favorite, whom she had executed the following day.

Jean Froissart, *Chronicles*, fol. 6r, France, 15th century
Bibliothèque Nationale de France, Paris; Français 2663

Unlike Jeanne de Clisson, the fourteenth-century military leader Joanna of Flanders, countess of Montfort, is found in a manuscript illumination. She is depicted in an account of the siege of Hennebont in 1342. Here she is seen carrying a lance on horseback out of the town—reflecting how Joanna personally led three hundred men against the besiegers, burning their supplies, and destroying their camp. This strike, alongside Joanna's practice of riding around the town in armor to rally the defenders, allowed her people to survive the siege until reinforcements could arrive.

Jean Froissart, *Chronicles*, fol. 87v, France, 15th century
Bibliothèque Nationale de France, Paris; Français 2663

Jeanne was incensed. Not only was her husband judicially murdered, but she too was accused of crimes against the French crown for her attempts to free him, and she was subsequently banished and her property confiscated.

Some women may have waited for their relatives to come to their aid, slowly working to gain pardons and the restitution of property over a potential period of years, but not Jeanne. After taking her sons to see their father's head on display in Nantes, she vowed retribution against the French king. She sold her husband's estates to raise money and used it to gather a force of several hundred loyal men. Together, they razed land in Brittany, attacking castles and garrisons. But this was not enough for Jeanne. Now gaining English support, she obtained three warships, which she had painted black, and hoisted red sails. As if that were not message enough, she named her flagship *My Revenge*. For years, her ships sailed the Channel targeting French ships, each time killing most of the crew and leaving just a few survivors to allow them to return to the French king with news of their attackers. Unsurprisingly, Jeanne gained the nickname "Lioness of Brittany." After well over a decade of piracy, having married for the final time to an English nobleman, Jeanne finally retired to a port town on the Brittany coast. She died just weeks after her husband, at the end of 1359, becoming a legend. Olivier's gruesome execution is illustrated in a copy of the *Chronicles* by fourteenth-century French historian Jean Froissart, but there are no images of Jeanne and her vengeful ways. Although her actions were supported by the men who followed her, and the English who benefited from them, for many contemporaries her behavior was

not something for women to emulate and thus was perhaps not seen as worthy of depicting in art, even if it was recorded in words.[38]

Women who were born into the nobility were lucky enough to live a much more privileged and luxurious life than most of society. By virtue of their birth, they were afforded a higher-quality education, and they were allowed to wield power and authority that was denied to women in most other aspects of life. Countries that had hereditary rulers ended up with a much higher proportion of women in positions of power, and women often found themselves as rulers in their own right. These women had to walk a fine line, however, to ensure they upheld their reputations. They had to display the correct attributes of femininity, or they could meet fierce resistance. But those who knew how to properly present themselves could find glory that long outlived them, going down in history for their piety, goodness, and mercy—especially if they encouraged this reputation by commissioning art that would outlive them.

As wealthy women, these nobles and royals could make their mark on the culture around them, patronizing artists and writers and building stunning monuments that would stand for centuries. Others shaped their world much more violently, picking up the sword to demand the changes they wanted or to bring vengeance on those who had wronged them. Noble and royal women have captured our imagination for the world of possibilities that was open to them and the ways in which they did not shy from taking up the challenge.

Though nobles usually had arranged marriages, love existed in many such unions. For a time in the late fourteenth century, tomb carvings of couples holding hands in a romantic gesture were popular.

Tomb of Thomas de Beauchamp and Katherine Mortimer, 14th century Saint Mary's Church, Warwick, England

IV. WRITERS AND ARTISTS

In an illustrated history of women in the Middle Ages, it seems only fitting to end by looking at the women writers and artists of the time. But defining who these women were is not necessarily straightforward. Artistic expression was, in many ways, viewed more fluidly than we might expect, and at the same time, some of these women would not have considered themselves as "writer" or "artist" as one would today.

For a large portion of the Middle Ages, most of the population was illiterate, but this did not mean that people could not "write"; scribes and notaries were common, and even those who could write would often dictate to others for ease, neatness, or conformity. This therefore opened writing to those who could not put quill to parchment themselves, whether because of illiteracy or disability. Many of these scribes would not have considered themselves writers as we define the profession today because they merely copied out manuscripts and did not write anything original themselves. But the illiterate writers and the scribes alike should be considered here, because knowing how to write in an age when it was not a given skill, or exercising the creative skills required in dictating a written work, should both be appreciated.

The oral culture of Europe in the Middle Ages needs to be examined further when we are looking at writers and artists, because it fundamentally affected the way medieval people approached these activities. As so many people could not read, written pieces were designed to be read aloud to an audience. Even in courtly circles where people could read, the performance of art was constant. From recitations of poets and minstrels to a crowd at a court function to chivalric romances being read aloud in a lady's chambers to her ladies-in-waiting, writing was rarely intended to be read silently by one person.

Monks and nuns in silent monasteries would have religious texts read to them during their meals for contemplation, and peasants would hear performances in public squares, taverns, and on other social occasions. These songs and stories were passed orally through generations until people began to write them down, and this shaped them over time. Various medieval texts reference women who "sing lullings and other cradle songs" to babies, and these early lullabies were written down and eventually transformed into carols, which invoked the Virgin Mary singing to baby Jesus.[1] In this way, women were vital in preserving and transmitting culture.

Master of the Cité des Dames (active c. 1400–1415); Master of the Duke of Bedford (active c. 1405–1465) Christine de Pisan, *Book of the Queen*, fol. 4r, France, c. 1414 Detail of page 163

↑ Women created tapestries both as a pastime and professionally. This intricate tapestry from a workshop in the southern Netherlands was skillfully made. It shows a variety of hunting scenes, with noblewomen depicted throughout.

The Devonshire Hunting Tapestry: Boar and Bear Hunt, southern Netherlands, 1430s
Wool, 14 ft. 7⅛ in. × 35 ft. 3½ in.
(4.45 × 10.76 m)
Victoria and Albert Museum, London

↗↗ Ancient Greek painter Timarete creates an image of the Virgin Mary and infant Jesus while a man grinds blue pigment for her to use. This painter's studio would have been familiar to medieval artists, as it was common for manuscript illuminations to show people from history in a contemporary setting.

Giovanni Boccaccio, *Des cleres et nobles femmes*, fol. 86r, France, 1401–1500
Bibliothèque Nationale de France, Paris;
Français 12420

Despite the popular depiction on television and film of the Middle Ages as a gray, dark, dull place, art was everywhere. Color was a marker of wealth and luxury, but peasants could also access a variety of dyes through local plant matter. Churches were filled with wall paintings and statues designed to both glorify God and educate the illiterate with biblical stories and moral warnings. Castles, which could be drafty with their stone walls, were covered interiorly in tapestries, rugs, and cushions to keep in warmth.

Participation in this culture of art was available to women of all levels. From the artists who painted religious portraits, the artisans who created the stained glass and tiles to decorate churches and palaces, the peasant women who sewed decorative cushions for their homes, and the nuns who wrote down their visions of heaven, to the queens who created intricate textiles to donate to religious institutions, women were at the heart of writing and art. Finding them, however, is another matter.

As with so many other aspects of medieval women's lives, it is difficult to definitively identify a woman as the creator of a piece of art. Many writers and artists did not record their names on their pieces, and even those who did can be difficult to find in other records. Some women gave plenty of information about themselves, and we still do not know who they were. The twelfth-century writer Marie de France recorded, in one of her epilogues, "Marie is my name /

I am from France," while a few decades later the writer Castelloza explains that she is from the Auvergne region in France and even names her husband, and yet historians are still unable to pin down their exact identities.[2] If we cannot identify those who left us explicit information, how can we begin to find those we know even less about? Time and again, though, women can be found in every European country in every century making art, and so it is important that we continue to consider that a portion of the countless anonymous pieces of surviving work must have been produced by women.

The final thing to consider is patronage. We saw in the last chapter that patronage was expected of royals and noblewoman, and their influence on the arts is not to be understated. Patrons did not just pay someone to construct a building or make a piece of jewelry but were often intimately involved in the design process. They would see drafts of poems or architectural plans and ask for changes in direction, or they might provide a clear vision for a tomb effigy that a sculptor would carry out. In the medieval mind, the patron "made" the item just as much as the maker did, and the patron's name was often recorded on an item as its maker, further complicating the task of identifying the actual craftsperson. There was no distinction between the designer and the manufacturer, as there would be today.[3] Though this chapter focuses on the actual makers of texts and artworks, the influence of female patrons is important to remember.

MISCELLANEOUS ARTS

Art comes in all shapes and formats, and before turning our attention to manuscripts and textiles, it's worth noting other types of art that involved women. We have already seen that female glaziers became more prevalent as the technology developed, enabling artistic glazier to become a separate profession from glassblower. As time went on, these advancements allowed for greater expression in glasswork, and women were closely involved in this process. Records from the 1440s onward refer to specialist glass painters who used enamel in their decoration, producing beautiful pieces in bright sapphire blues, emerald greens, and aubergine purples. Throughout the second half of the fifteenth century and into the early sixteenth century, fourteen of these specialist painters can be found in Venetian records, and two women were among this elite group.

It may be unsurprising to find that these two women came from established glassmaking families. Elena de Laudo operated at least during the 1440s and had blank panes of glass delivered to her for painting. Several of her family members were also painters, and at least one is identified as having painted a window for one of Venice's churches.[4] A few decades later, Marietta Barovier, another Venetian woman from a leading and well-established glassmaking family, made a name for herself. Her father, Angelo Barovier, who was said by one poet to be "endowed with angelic powers" for his talent, had invented *cristallo* around 1455, a highly sought-after crystal-clear glass. When he died in 1460, his daughter Marietta and her brother Giovanni inherited the family workshop.

Marietta had obviously learned well under her father, for she too excelled among Venetian glassmakers. In 1487, she was given the privilege of constructing a special kiln—the ownership of furnaces

↘ This dish, which may have been used as a decoration or as a basin for washing hands, is adorned with the head and bust of a woman.

Dish, Italy (Bologna), 1480–1500
Red earthenware covered with white slip, incised, and painted, diameter: 13⅛ in. (33.3 cm)
Victoria and Albert Museum, London; C.2283-1910

→→ As nobles began to create grand funeral monuments, it became popular to place small statues of weeping mourners, often depictions of family members, around their tombs. This woman adorned the tomb of Isabella of Bourbon, Duchess of Burgundy, which Isabella's daughter Mary had built after her death. Tomb monuments not only depicted women but were often commissioned and designed by them too.

Borman workshop (active 15th–16th centuries); casting by Renier van Thienen (c. 1460–c. 1541) (attributed)
Female Weeper Wearing a Large Linen Cap, Belgium (Brussels), 1475–76
Bronze, 23¼ × 8⅜ × 5¼ in. (59 × 21.5 × 13.5 cm)
Rijksmuseum, Amsterdam

→→→ The Dynna Stone, erected by Gunnvor in memory of her daughter Astrid, provides an excellent example of how medieval women could use art to shape the world around them and to ensure their legacy would be remembered forever.

Dynna Stone (detail), Norway, 11th century
Sandstone with runic inscriptions, height: approx. 118⅛ in. (300 cm)
Kulturhistorisk Museum, Oslo

↘↘ Female sculptors are hard to track down in written records, but they were still portrayed in art.

Robinet Testard (active c. 1471–1531)
Giovanni Boccaccio, *Des cleres et nobles femmes*, fol. 58r, France, 1488–96
Bibliothèque Nationale de France, Paris; Français 599

being fiercely regulated by glassmakers—for making her "beautiful, unusual and not blown works." At the start of the decade, Marietta had also invented the rosette, or chevron, bead, which became the iconic glass bead of Venice.[5] Her success shows that women were not always mere assistants in artistic crafts but could in fact be the spearhead of their profession.

On the opposite side of Europe and at the opposite end of the Middle Ages, another woman had become renowned for her craft. Astrid lived in the first half of the eleventh century in Norway. Almost nothing is known of her other than that she was "the handiest maiden in Hadeland," known for her "nimble fingers." The exact nature of her craft has been lost, but suggestions have ranged from textiles to stone carvings to jewelry.[6] The only reason we know of Astrid's existence is because she was commemorated after her death by her mother, Gunnvor, who erected a bridge and a runestone in Astrid's memory; the runestone contains the inscription exalting her artistic skills.

Gunnvor's runestone not only praises her daughter but also contains one of the earliest pictorial Christian scenes in Scandinavian art. Astrid and Gunnvor lived in the Viking age at a time when Christianity was gaining prominence, but old traditions held even as they merged with the new religion. The stone has the Epiphany and the Nativity carved into it, and the bridge erected alongside the memorial has given rise to the suggestion that the imagery of the Magi being guided by the star was chosen purposefully to complement the way the bridge would have guided travelers.[7] Gunnvor's runestone served a plethora of purposes. It commemorated her daughter and also signified their status in the local community, for only families of high social standing could afford to commission such projects; constructing a bridge would also bolster the family's status since it could support the good of the community. Runestones were also important ways of ensuring inheritance by claiming family ties and their connection to the land. Finally, considering the conversion of Norway began around 1000, this early Christian runestone was a statement to anyone who saw it of Gunnvor's—and, by association, Astrid's—adoption of the new religion. With the construction of what has become known as the Dynna Stone, both Gunnvor's and Astrid's participation in the arts has been commemorated for a millennium.

Women not only commissioned monuments but also were sometimes involved in their production. While we have less evidence of female sculptors than other artistic trades, they do crop up occasionally. The Paris tax rolls between 1292 and 1316 list two women, Aalis and Perronelle, as sculptors.[8] It is also clear that women helped in the workshops of sculptors. But finding names remains difficult, and even when they appear, they can be obfuscated by legend and misinterpretation. In the nineteenth century, historians thought they had discovered a female sculptor named Sabina von Steinbach, who allegedly carved some beautiful stone statues on the outside of the cathedral of Notre-Dame in Strasbourg, France. Sabina, operating in the early fourteenth century, was supposedly identified by an inscription on one of the statues and assumed to be the daughter

of Erwin von Steinbach, a stonemason and sculptor who has been linked to the cathedral. The alleged inscription was subsequently lost, yet legend continued to run with this rarely identified female sculptor until recently, when historians pointed out that the statues attributed to Sabina were carved about forty years before Erwin himself worked on the cathedral.[9]

TEXTILES

Textiles were among the most important commodities in the Middle Ages. The demand for the luxurious silk of the East led to the flourishing trade along the Silk Road, and England and the Low Countries had their own booms in woolen textiles due to the high value of English wool and the skillful processing by their neighbors across the water. We have already seen that women were involved in the manufacturing of textiles from raw materials into threads and cloths. But women were also involved in the process in a more artistic way through their creation of finished products.

Women of all levels of society were expected to be skilled seamstresses. Peasants needed to make and repair their own clothes, professionals needed to create products for the lucrative markets, and noblewomen needed to show off their skill with a needle to exemplify their feminine virtues. Toward the end of the Middle Ages, it became increasingly popular to depict the Virgin Mary weaving at a loom or embroidering fabric, demonstrating the virtue of such work. Working with textiles was a way to keep idleness at bay by dedicating oneself to a beautiful and useful task. Its importance was consistently promoted to nuns, who could take up the needle to show their devotion to God and also pass their time in an appropriately feminine way. In 1240, during a visitation to the convent of Heiningen in Germany, it was recommended that the nuns should work with textiles. The nuns took up this suggestion, and a linen altar cloth they created around two decades later still survives today. The cloth was inscribed with the names of the founders of the convent and local patron saints, demonstrating the skills of the makers' hands alongside their piety.[10] Two centuries later, the bishop of Eichstätt in Bavaria said that while feast days should be spent entirely in prayer, nuns were exempt, "as women they are not skilled at continually reading Holy Scripture." This duty, he suggested, "can be converted into handiwork, so as to avoid idleness and gossip."[11]

Some of the textiles nuns created were for their personal use in their quarters or cloisters, but they also made altar cloths for their associated churches and vestments for priests to wear, and these could also be sent to other institutions and parish churches. The nuns' work was highly valued, and special pieces were often reserved for feast days or for the most important men in the church; when King Henry II of England sent ambassadors to Pope Adrian IV to request permission to invade Ireland, he sent a collection of gifts, but the only ones the pope accepted were three beautifully embroidered miters (ceremonial headdresses) created by the famous English prioress Christina of Markyate.[12] Some people specially commissioned

German nuns became known for white-on-white embroidery, some of which was actually originally made with colored thread. Several pieces created by the nuns of the monastery at Altenberg, Germany, beautifully demonstrate this skill. We know the names of the nuns who embroidered the altar cloth currently housed at the Metropolitan Museum of Art (*left*)—Sophia, Hadewigis, and Lucardis—as they stitched their names into the border of the cloth.

↑ Nuns of Altenberg Abbey
Altar cloth, Germany, c. 1350
Embroidered linen, 60¾ × 147⅜ in.
(154.3 × 374.5 cm)
Cleveland Museum of Art

← Sophia, Hadewigis, and Lucardis (nuns of Altenberg Abbey)
Altar cloth, Germany, 1350–1400
Embroidered linen, 47½ × 156 in.
(120.7 × 396.2 cm)
Metropolitan Museum of Art, New York

←← The central image of this textile depicts
the Crucifixion (contrast enhanced).
Detail of pages 150–51 (*top*)

↑   The inscribed names "Sophia"
and "Hadewigis" faintly appear
along the bottom border of this
image (contrast enhanced).
Detail of page 150 (*bottom*)

This frontal band for an altar, made by Joanna of Beverly, is the only surviving English embroidered piece from the medieval period on which the maker's name is sewn. Her name (pictured above the finished textile) was inscribed with black thread, and is only discerned by the holes where the stitches were made.

Joanna of Beverly (active 14th century)
Altar frontal band (details), England, 1300–1350
Embroidered linen, 3⅞ × 102⅞ in. (10 × 261.5 cm)
Victoria and Albert Museum, London

nuns for the quality of their work, as Icelandic bishop Vilchin did in the late fourteenth century when he ordered tapestries from the nuns in Kirkjubæjarklaustur for the cathedral in Skálholt. Of fifteen surviving antependiums, or altar frontals, from medieval Iceland, at least six are believed to have been made in the Reynistaðarklaustur nunnery alone, demonstrating the value of the nuns' craft.[13]

Embroidery demonstrates not only the nuns' skill with a needle but also their exemplary education. Complicated biblical and classical subjects were frequently depicted on their cloths, as the nuns from the convent of Quedlinburg in Germany exhibited in a thirteenth-century tapestry that showed the marriage of Mercury and Philology. In a visual society, textiles could also serve as important records— around 1200, the prioress and two nuns of the monastery of Lothen, also in Germany, wove numerous tapestries that as a whole told the story of the monastery's history.[14] The output of nuns could be impressive: between 1492 and 1508, the nuns of the convent of Lüne in Germany worked tirelessly to create at least seven woolen embroideries, which survive today and amount to some 915 square feet (85 square meters). Over those sixteen years, seventeen nuns worked on the project, and they signed their work with their initials.[15]

These groups of German nuns became renowned across Europe for a particular style of embroidery known today as the white-on-white technique because it survives as colorless linen threads on white linen backgrounds, somewhat obscuring the skillful depictions of people, animals, ornaments, and inscriptions. However, recent research has shown that at least some of these embroideries were originally done in threads colored with dark blue or brown dye, which has faded into white over time.[16]

England, known for its high-quality wool, also became famous for its inhabitants' own skills in embroidery from the thirteenth

The Butler-Bowdon Cope is one of the
finest examples of an English textile from
the Middle Ages—it is an early example
of woven silk velvet, which was still new
in Europe. The embroidery on the cope
(a liturgical vestment) was created using
gold, silver, and colored silks, delicately
embellished with pearls and glass beads.
The scenes down the center show events
from the life of the Virgin Mary, while the
rest of the cope is decorated with various
apostles, saints, and angels. It is not known
who created this beautiful piece, but nuns
certainly made liturgical vestments like this.

Butler-Bowdon Cope, England, 1330–50
Embroidered silk velvet with metallic
and silk threads, pearls, and glass beads,
63¾ × 113 in. (162 × 287 cm)
Victoria and Albert Museum, London

Englishwomen became known across
Europe for their embroidery skills, and their
work took on the name *opus Anglicanum*
as a signifier of this talent. This burse, used to
carry a liturgical cloth to the altar, is one
of the earliest surviving examples of opus
Anglicanum. It shows two female saints,
Margaret and Catherine.

Burse, England, 1335–45
Embroidered silk velvet with
metallic thread, 10⅞ × 11⅛ in.
(27.7 × 28.2 cm)
Victoria and Albert Museum, London

→→ Women can be found even in pieces
of art meant to commemorate the
deeds of men. The Bayeux Tapestry,
an extensive narrative embroidery
that records the Norman Conquest
of England, depicts just three women
in its fifty-eight scenes. One is fleeing
a burning house; one is thought to
be Queen Edith, the wife of Edward
the Confessor and the sister of King
Harold; and the third is the woman
shown here, known only by her name,
Aelfgyva. Pictured with a priest, she is
the only woman named on the tapestry,
and though the meaning of the scene
has been lost, it must have been a very
famous event to have been depicted
on the tapestry. In such examples, art
can provide us with clues lost from the
written record.

Bayeux Tapestry (detail), England,
c. 1070
Wool embroidery on linen,
c. 27½ in. × 224 ft. (70 cm × 68.3 m)
Musée de la Tapisserie, Bayeux, France

↘ ↘ Scandinavian women were appreciated
for their skills with tapestries, which
were important cultural items valued for
their preservation of history as much
as for their artistry. This section of the
Skog Tapestry shows figures inside a
church ringing its bells.

Skog Tapestry (detail), Sweden,
13th century
Woven linen and wool, c. 13¾ × 68⅞ in.
(35 × 175 cm)
Statens Historiska Museum, Stockholm

century onward. Pope Adrian was not alone in recognizing the women's skill in the gifts he received. The women undertaking this work were so accomplished in designing and executing their embroideries that across Europe their pieces were highly sought after and known by the name *opus Anglicanum* (English work). Despite the plethora of opus Anglicanum pieces that survive today, their creators remain largely unknown. Only one signed piece of English medieval embroidery is known, an embroidered prayer reading "in hora mortis sucurre nobis domine" (In the hour of death hasten to help us, O Lord) on one side and signed "domna johanna beverlai monaca me fecit" (Lady Joanna of Beverly, a Nun, Made Me) on the other, as seen on page 154.[17]

By this time, England had a long history of talented women embroiderers. The famous Bayeux Tapestry of the eleventh century, though probably designed by men, likely involved professional female embroiderers. Despite its French name, the tapestry is thought to have been created in England, and the women living there before the Norman Conquest were renowned for their skill. In 1016, records show, Queen Ælfgifu was embroidering an exquisite altar frontal studded with gold, pearls, and gems. The Domesday Book, a land survey from the same century, notes several women who had kept their positions in the new Norman regime because of their skills with a needle. One, Leofgyd, had an estate in Wiltshire "because she used to make, and still makes, the embroidery of the King and Queen," while another, Aelfgyd, received some land from the sheriff of Buckinghamshire in return for teaching his daughter embroidery.[18]

The design of textiles could be an important medium for recording changes in wider culture. The nuns of Lothen showed how textiles could record history, but for women in Scandinavia, textiles could also commemorate shifts in religion. Just as the Dynna Stone bridged Norse culture and the new Christian religion, so too could women's textile work record this change with a needle and thread. Scandinavian culture placed a high value on textiles as an art form, and their importance as a record is demonstrated by the word *bók*, which translates as both "book" and "tapestry."

As women typically were the first adopters of Christianity, it makes sense that early depictions of Christian iconography came from the types of work most frequently produced by women. The Skog Tapestry, created in the thirteenth century, depicts a church with a cross and a bell tower filled with people. Art is very much interpretive, and this tapestry has caused considerable debate. Its depictions have been read by some as a metaphorical battle between Christianity and Nordic paganism.[19] Part of it shows three figures that were initially thought to represent Norse gods, as one had only a single eye like the god Odin. But research has since shown that the figure originally had a second eye, which has just been lost to the sands of time, leading to new suggestions that the three could represent biblical figures such as the Magi instead. Scandinavian pieces like the Skog Tapestry tended to be created using the *soumak* technique, which creates a flat pattern by weaving overlapping threads across the warp at an angle.

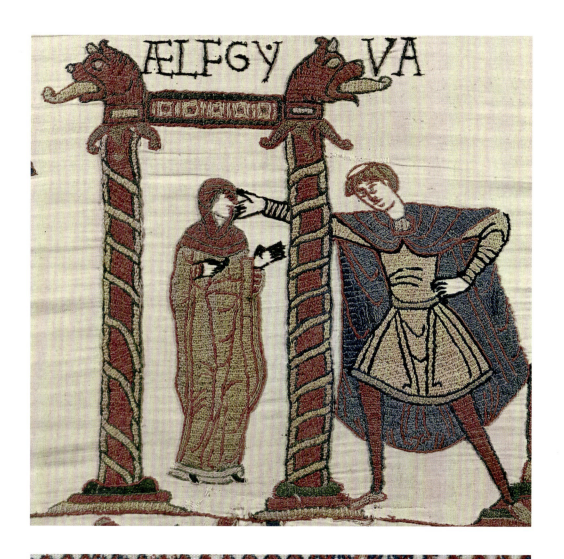

ÆLFGYVA

All over Europe, women were engaged both at an individual level and in groups to create pieces of art using a variety of textile techniques. These pieces adorned bodies, covered walls and floors, and decorated soft furnishings, and their creators gained accolades and were exalted across Europe for their individual styles and skills.

TROUBADOURS AND POETS

Over time, the art of the written word became as important as visual media to medieval Europeans. Since much of Europe was illiterate for a large part of the Middle Ages, written work was made more accessible through oral performance. When writers wrote, they had in mind that their text would be read aloud to groups of people as often as it was read by an individual, if not more so. Writing was therefore expected to entertain as much as educate, and chronicle histories were written with almost as much dialogue and flair as chivalric romances.

Troubadours knew this better than anyone. Composers and performers of poetry, troubadours originated in the Occitan culture in the south of France, particularly Aquitaine and Provence, and spread to nearby regions in Spain, Portugal, and Italy. While similar groups eventually spread across Europe, the high period for the troubadours in those territories was from the 1170s to the 1210s. The troubadours were very much a subculture but one that was inclusive of women. Female troubadours, often known as *trobairitz*, were quite visible during this period, and a handful of the most famous were also memorialized in manuscript art.

Troubadours and trobairitz proliferated in these southern courts. Their songs followed emerging ideas of chivalry and courtly love and were often romantic verses written from the perspective of an admirer to the object of affection. The Occitan was particularly conducive to the open participation of women in this art because women there experienced quite significant freedoms during this time. The region had more favorable laws toward women, was much more tolerant of female inheritance, and extensive lands were owned by women. Aquitaine was ruled by a duchess, the infamous Eleanor of Aquitaine, for almost seventy years (from 1137 until her death in 1204), which coincided with troubadour culture. The region was also experiencing a period of economic and cultural expansion that gave its people time to enjoy the arts.[20]

Trobairitz, like troubadours, were expected to perform their pieces to the court. Although authorship is often unknown, this more

← ← Nuns created stunning embroideries that were usually religious in nature to hang in their convents or to gift to others. This colorful embroidery is thought to have been created by a convent of nuns in Hildesheim, Lower Saxony, because it depicts saints that the nuns there venerated.

Embroidered hanging, Germany, 1350–1400
Silk on linen with painted inscriptions, 63 × 62½ in. (160 × 158.8 cm)
Metropolitan Museum of Art, Cloisters, New York

↙ Noblewomen were expected to have skills, such as playing a musical instrument, to entertain at court. For a time, a handful of nobles became *trobairitz* (female troubadours), which required talent not only in music and performance but also in writing ballads to perform to crowds.

Robinet Testard (active c. 1471–1531)
Evrart de Conty, *Le Livre des échecs amoureux moralisés*, fol. 65v, France, 1496–98
Bibliothèque Nationale de France, Paris; Français 143

→ Eleanor of Aquitaine was the only woman to be both queen of France and queen of England, but she was also duchess of Aquitaine in her own right. Her rule of Aquitaine lasted for almost seventy years, during which time trobairitz flourished in the region.

Tomb of Eleanor of Aquitaine (detail), 1204–10
Stone, 92⅝ × 29½ in. (235.3 × 75.1 cm)
Fontevrault Abbey, France

↘ This portrait in a manuscript initial depicts a famous trobairitz, the Countess of Dia.

Provençal Song (detail), fol. 126v, Italy (Padua–Venice), 13th century
Bibliothèque Nationale de France, Paris; Français 12473

→→ An aristocratic woman plays a stringed instrument on a Germanic playing card in a scene reminiscent of the trobairitz phenomenon.

Virgin (Six) from the so-called Court Office Game, Austria (Vienna?), c. 1445
Paper, woodcut, watercolor, and ink, 5½ × 3⅞ in. (13.9 × 9.9 cm)
Kunsthistorisches Museum, Vienna

↘↘ Although the identity of the writer Marie de France remains unknown, she must have been popular in her time to have been the subject of this beautiful miniature made with gold leaf, which depicts her writing at her desk.

Collection of old French poetry, fol. 256r, France, 1275–1300
Bibliothèque Nationale de France, Paris; Ms-3142

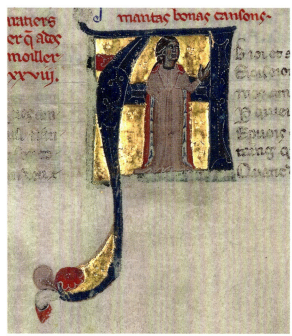

public culture means that we do know of many women performers' names. There are about twenty-seven hundred surviving troubadour songs, and around twenty trobairitz have been identified by historians. It is therefore safe to presume that a reasonable proportion of the surviving songs with unknown attribution would have been written by women.[21]

Due to the nature of their work—requiring the writer to be literate, well versed in her genre in order to follow (or know how to break) convention, and have access to a court—plenty of trobairitz were from the upper classes. The earliest troubadour work to survive is by Duke William IX of Aquitaine, who lived from the end of the eleventh century and into the first quarter of the twelfth century, and he was not the only aristocrat to pick up a quill. One of the most famous trobairitz was the Countess of Dia, who is depicted in various manuscripts. It was common for troubadours to have *vidas*, or "lives," written about them, ostensibly their biographies, much in the same way as religious women. But, just as one may expect a saint's *vita* to twist or exaggerate the truth in order to emphasize its subject's holiness, there is evidence that these troubadour vidas were often fictionalized. If the countess's vida is to be believed, then she was Beatriz, wife of William of Poitiers, Count of Valentinois—but she fell in love with fellow troubadour Raimbaut III, Lord of Orange and Aumelas.[22]

The themes explored by troubadours and trobairitz centered on love, which allowed female writers to play with perhaps shocking perspectives on the subject. In a time when, ostensibly, women were supposed to marry, be devoted and loyal wives, and birth many children, the trobairitz songs explored other views. The Countess of Dia was not the only trobairitz said to have been married to one man but in love with another. A trobairitz known as Lady Carenza advises two young sisters to disregard love and marriage and instead focus on the "Crown of Wisdom." Another, named Bieiris de Romans, wrote a love poem addressed to a fellow woman named Maria.[23] How true to life the descriptions of these woman and the views espoused in their poetry are, or whether they were simply following an accepted romantic, courtly formula, is unclear. But their participation in the genre certainly demonstrates the freedom of

expression that was available to the women of Occitan for a period of time.

Thanks to the work of the trobairitz, other female poets and writers found a place in medieval Europe. One of the most significant was Marie de France, who was the first known woman to compose vernacular narrative poetry in Europe.[24] As already mentioned, although Marie provided some information about herself, her identity remains obscured. It is clear that Marie was highly educated, fluent in at least French and Latin and familiar with English, and that she was a very popular writer. Although only three confirmed pieces by Marie survive today, these works were translated into a significant number of languages—from Norse to Italian—showing the geographic spread of her writing. It also seems that Marie's popularity aroused some jealousy and inspired copycats, for in the epilogue to one of her works, she writes, "It may be that many clerks / will take my labor on themselves— / I don't want any of them to claim it."

Marie felt that the educated had a moral duty to share their knowledge with others. She appears to have recorded pieces of Breton songs and stories among her poetry, making folk tradition available in print for the first time. She translated *Saint Patrick's Purgatory*, an extensive Latin work that runs to twenty-three hundred lines, into French in order to make it more accessible; and she also wrote a collection of 102 fables, which she called *Ysopet*, or "Little Aesop," as they were her twists on the classical Aesop's Fables, alongside newly recorded fables that might have had origins in folktales or legends from the East.[25]

The influence of trobairitz and poets spread into Spain, as Frenchwomen brought their culture with them when they moved to the country. Violant of Bar, a granddaughter of King Jean II of France, married the heir of the Aragonese throne in 1380. The couple became king and queen by the end of the decade, and Violant exerted significant influence over the culture of the Aragonese court. Upon her arrival, she introduced the French culture she had grown up with, bringing courtly love games, the reading of French literature, and introducing French artists and poets.[26] Although the work of very few Spanish women writers survives today, which suggests a more hostile culture to female participation than the trobairitz had found in southern France, the legacy of female patrons like Violant certainly helped pave the way for certain women writers; a century later, Florencia Pinar found work at the court of the joint monarchs Ferdinand and Isabella by writing erotic love poetry.[27]

WRITERS

As the Middle Ages progressed, the preference for vernacular languages over Latin and the language of the elite became more prevalent. In some European countries, the nobility used one language, and the rest of society used another, as in England, where English was the language of the masses while the court and government used French as well as Latin. As bureaucrats started to favor the

vernacular in their official records, so too did authors of other pieces of writing. This made writing far more accessible to women, who were less likely to be educated to the same level as men. Once poems, stories, chronicles, and all other forms of written media became more commonly expressed in the native tongue, the frequency of female writers increased.

Manuscripts had always been valued for the incredible labor and cost that went into creating them, and rising literacy by around the thirteenth century only increased their demand. As more and more books poured into the market in the vernacular and in entertaining formats rather than heavy religious or philosophical tomes, an upward spiral in book production both fed—and was fed by—this increasing audience. This market exploded upon the invention of the printing press, which allowed for mass production, and went in hand with the increasing availability of paper imported from China. These new technologies allowed for cheaper and more portable books than the vellum volumes of the preceding centuries.[28]

Perhaps the most famous female writer of the Middle Ages was Christine de Pisan, considered the first professional woman writer in Europe. An incredible corpus of Christine's work survives today. Her writing was treasured and widely disseminated, leaving us with a trove of beautifully illuminated manuscripts that often feature portraits of Christine at work. Christine was born in the 1360s in Venice, and when she was a child, her father, known for his astrological skills, was invited to the court of Charles V of France. He accepted, and brought his family with him. When Christine was around fifteen years old, she married a royal secretary, but she was widowed a decade later and left with three children. Her father had died just a year prior, and so Christine, a woman only in her mid-twenties, was left to care for herself, her children, and her mother.

Christine had been educated, so she turned to writing for the French court that she knew so well as a way to support her family. She began by writing poetry, reflecting on her life circumstances as a lonely widow, but she was soon influenced by the court around her. She became more political and is sometimes considered an early feminist (a problematic framing), as she often turned her hand to defending the female sex. She drew from biblical examples as well as from women in history to provide evidence that women were capable, virtuous, strong, and deserving of admiration. This culminated in her most famous works, *The Book of the City of Ladies* and *The Treasure of the City of Ladies*, in which she both defends women and provides them with an instruction manual for how to properly conduct themselves.

Although Christine's works applied to women of all social statuses, she particularly wanted to direct future female rulers: the princesses, countesses, duchesses, and ladies of Europe who, as wives, mothers, regents, and rulers in their own right, would significantly influence the world around them. Christine exhorted them to be paragons of womanhood, feared and respected for their perfect displays of femininity. Her works were wildly popular and

Writers and scribes often had special desks that allowed them to consult multiple manuscripts at once while they were writing, as in this image.

Master of Berry's Cleres Femmes (active c. 1404–1415); Master of the Coronation of the Virgin (active 1399–1405)
Giovanni Boccaccio, *De claris mulieribus*, fol. 143v, France, 1403
Bibliothèque Nationale de France, Paris; Français 598

were translated across Europe for centuries. Men and women of the highest echelons of society sought commissions from her, for her knowledge and writing skills were not solely limited to the female sex; Philip, Duke of Burgundy, requested she write a history of King Charles V of France, while an unknown patron asked her to write *The Book of Feats of Arms and of Chivalry*, a manual on conducting warfare seemingly intended for the French dauphin.[29] That a woman was considered able to instruct a prince in such a subject demonstrates the respect her writing was granted.

In Christian Europe, religious writings were just as popular as secular ones. As much as people enjoyed poetry, romances, and stories of heroic deeds, they were also interested in caring for their spiritual health. It was expected that nobles would have various religious books, from primers (prayer books) to lives of saints, and as literacy spread, these texts became more common lower down the social ladder as well. We have already touched upon the writings of European mystics, a genre that spread the visions of nuns to the masses. Pioneers of the genre include Beatrice of Nazareth and Hadewijch, two renowned Dutch writers in the first half of the thirteenth century. Beatrice holds the accolade of being the second Dutch literary author known by name (the first was Heinrich von Veldeke), but both she and Hadewijch wrote in the vernacular in an innovative way.[30] Though these two women were clearly highly educated and skilled writers, they chose to write in Dutch to better connect with their fellow countrymen and countrywomen.

Marie de France asserted that "whoever has received knowledge / and eloquence in speech from God / should not be silent or conceal it / but demonstrate it willingly." Medieval mystics likewise believed it was their duty to share their visions with the world.[31] We have seen that these visions were often transcribed through the medium of a male priest, and though this helped protect women from accusations of heresy, toward the end of the Middle Ages this also was a means for illiterate women to access writing. A woman could now become a writer by dictating her words.

Margery Kempe was one of medieval England's most famous mystics, though she never became a nun and is surprisingly absent from contemporary artwork. Living from the late fourteenth century and to the mid-fifteenth century, Margery was a merchant's daughter who led a typical life, marrying and having at least fourteen children, before she found herself called to Christ through her visions. This eventually led her to form a chaste relationship with her husband and devote herself to Christianity in a way not dissimilar to the lifestyle of the beguines. In the 1430s, Margery dictated her biography, first to a scribe and then, when he died with the work unfinished, to a priest. This work was the first autobiography written in English. Though Margery was illiterate, she had memorized scripture and prayers as well as important spiritual texts, and she was able to weave this knowledge into references in her book.[32] Visionary writing became a way for mystics to access theological respect traditionally denied to them as women, as they could claim that their knowledge and thoughts came not from themselves but from God.

Though Margery was not a nun, many who took the veil used the opportunity of their learning and access to a corpus of works to write a variety of texts both for use in their convents and to be disseminated to the wider community. Constanza of Castile, royal prioress of Santo Domingo el Real de Madrid, wrote a personal book of prayers for her nuns to use. The prayers written by Mechtild of Hackeborn, a nun from Helfta, Germany, were recited by Florentine citizens during religious rituals. Nuns of the convent of the Poor Clares in Cologne produced collections of musical manuscripts.[33] Writing was at the heart of countless female religious institutions across Europe. Even when old age and health conditions affected these women, they continued to write. Mechtild of Magdeburg was a German mystic who wrote numerous religious tracts, but as she grew older, she lost her eyesight and eventually became blind. This did not stop her passion, however, for she dictated her final book of revelations to her fellow nuns.[34]

Both secular and religious women writers had strong motivations, whether it was to participate in the cultural milieu of their court, to spread the word of God, or to provide for their families. Female patrons shared these motivations and had just as strong an influence on the production of the written word. As we saw in the previous chapter, noble and royal women could direct the style and topics of literature in their spheres of influence. While this often reflected the women's personal tastes, it was also done extremely purposefully to ensure one's legacy and that of their family. Philippa of Hainault, for instance, commissioned a poet to write an elegy

Helene Kottanner wrote her memoirs
to tell the world of her part in
the dramatic events that unfolded
as she assisted Queen Elizabeth
of Luxembourg in the contested
leadership of the Kingdom of Hungary.
Though an image of Helene does not
survive, this manuscript drawing shows
Elizabeth (*bottom center*; crowned, in
green) with her mother, Barbara of
Cilli, Holy Roman empress (*bottom
right*; crowned, in brown). It was
created at roughly the same time as
Elizabeth's struggles.

Ulrich von Richenthal, *Chronicle of
the Council of Constance*, fol. 44v,
Germany, c. 1440
Österreichische Nationalbibliothek,
Vienna; Cod. 3044

for her father a few years after his death.[35] No short piece of work,
Li *regret Guillaume* has a ninety-six-line opening. By paying a poet to
create a piece like this, Philippa was not only honoring her father's
legacy but also boosting the reputation of her entire family and recording their glory for posterity.

Female patrons also supported female writers, and this relationship could be mutually beneficial. Isabeau of Bavaria had been queen
of France since 1385, but since the early 1390s her husband, Charles
VI, had suffered from mental illnesses that left him incapable of
ruling for extended periods of time. Though Isabeau acted as regent
in various periods, by the 1410s, civil war had broken out among the
French royal family, with different branches vying for control while
the king was incapacitated. Isabeau recognized the importance of
written works in bolstering one's reputation, and she requested
that a beautifully decorated collection of Christine de Pisan's works
be created for her, the last piece being *The Book of the City of Ladies*.

Christine ensured the artist of the manuscript, known as the Book of the Queen, included a miniature portrait of herself presenting the completed volume to Isabeau (an image we saw in the previous chapter; see page 102).

Christine had long been a supporter of Isabeau, and various parts of the City of Ladies, completed a decade prior to the Book of the Queen, supported her right to regency by referencing women from French history who had governed well and speaking favorably of Isabeau throughout the text. Isabeau's commission for the new compilation of Christine's work arrived in early 1414, just as her chancellor was arguing in the royal council that Isabeau should be leading the government of France.[36] In this example, we see cycles of support created between female patron and female writer, the latter finding paid employment while the former obtained propaganda supporting her right to exert power.

In some cases, women would even write to explicitly glorify their own actions. Helene Kottanner was born around 1400 in Sopron, Hungary, into a family of lesser nobles. In 1436, Helene entered royal service as a nurse to Princess Elizabeth. She soon became the confidante of the princess's mother, Queen Elizabeth of Luxembourg, wife of Albert II, the king of Germany, Hungary, Croatia, and Bohemia. Albert died three years after Helene entered royal service, and she found herself suddenly thrust into the greatest events of her time. Queen Elizabeth had given birth to two daughters with Albert, and she was pregnant when he died. An interregnum was declared as the kingdoms waited to see whether Elizabeth would give birth to a son.

Elizabeth was keen to protect the rights of her child, whom she was convinced was a boy, but men around her were vying for control. The nobles of the council wanted Elizabeth to swiftly marry King Wladislaus III of Poland, who had his own claims to the territories, but Elizabeth did not wish to. Around a decade later, Helene wrote her memoirs recounting her key role in what happened next, and the Denkwürdigkeiten, as she called them, are considered the oldest memoirs written by a woman in the Middle Ages.

Elizabeth fled the court with her followers and retreated to give birth. She then made a significant request of Helene: that she steal the Holy Crown of Hungary, with which all kings of Hungary had been crowned since the twelfth century, and bring it to Elizabeth. Helene's memoirs recount her harrowing task and the significant danger she was in by participating in this scheme. Helene was ultimately successful and managed to bring the crown to Elizabeth on the same day that she gave birth. The baby was indeed a boy, and Elizabeth had him swiftly coronated with the Holy Crown, cementing his position as king—and hers as regent.[37] Helene explains that she was Elizabeth's sole confidante, whom the queen trusted without question, and was the only one who could pull off such a heist.

Helene wrote her memoirs eleven years after the events recounted, and their creation was likely spurred by the political situation at the time. Elizabeth's son, Ladislaus, was at the center of a conflict over the administration of his guardianship, which had been extended

until he was eighteen years old. However, many Hungarian lords believed he should take over as king when he turned twelve. Helene may have been attempting to assert Ladislaus's legitimate claim to the throne by recounting her tale, though shortly after the release of the memoirs, she received a reward from the regent of Hungary in the form of a grant of a village for her role in stealing the crown, possibly highlighting personal motives. Helene had inadvertently stepped into a significant, ongoing controversy in her country, and by becoming a writer and telling her own story, she had made a choice to set the record straight while also protecting her own legacy and that of her old friend, the queen.

PERCEPTIONS OF FEMALE READERS AND WRITERS

As reading became more common among the general populace, its portrayal in art became more widespread. Whereas the Virgin Mary frequently had been depicted with textiles, engaged in weaving or spinning, she was increasingly shown reading. The virtues of knowledge and literacy were seen as important attributes for the

↖ Through the medieval period, it became more common to educate girls. This is reflected in the art of the period— especially in devotional books of hours, like this one—which increasingly depicted the Virgin Mary as a child being taught to read by her mother, Saint Anne. These holy women acted as models for ordinary women.

Master of Sir John Fastolf
(active c. 1420–1460)
Book of hours, fol. 45v, England or France, 1430–40
Getty, Los Angeles; Ms. 5

↑ This painting of the Virgin Mary is rare for the Middle Ages as it depicts her writing (albeit with the guidance of the baby Jesus and the supervision of angels). The painting reflects changing attitudes and an increasing acceptance in Italian society that some women were able writers.

Sandro Botticelli (1444/45–1510)
Madonna of the Magnificat, Italy, c. 1483
Tempera on wood, diameter: 46⅜ in.
(118 cm)
Le Gallerie degli Uffizi, Florence

Mother of God, and the significance of women as early teachers also grew as time went on. From the fourteenth century, the idea evolved that Mary's mother, Anne, had been her teacher, and depictions of Anne instructing Mary to read spread across Europe. As the medieval period drew to a close, Mary is eventually seen writing in some pieces of art. Though intended to show her exceptionalism among women, it unwittingly highlighted an increasing acceptance of female writers.[38]

This was not a universal opinion, however. Invariably, men questioned why women needed to read and write beyond a certain level—and especially women of the lower classes. The need for noble and royal women to have those abilities was clear, as they were expected to rule territories and support their husbands. But as the Middle Ages progressed, and women from knightly and mercantile classes became more literate, many men became uncomfortable with the implications of this. It was recognized that it was useful for a woman to have a degree of literacy so that she could read the Bible and other religious texts for the good of her soul, but many questioned the value of a woman being educated beyond this level.

These conflicting ideas, based on class and gender, often led to situations where individual women were extolled for their uniqueness and praised while other women were simultaneously disparaged. Fifteenth-century Italy was particularly fertile ground for this contradiction. This period, known as the quattrocento, is when the Renaissance begins. As Renaissance humanism developed, it became popular, particularly in northern Italy, for men of the movement to educate their daughters to a much higher degree than was done elsewhere in Europe. These noble and bourgeois women were taught to read and write; received instruction in several languages, usually Latin but also Greek and even Hebrew; and learned about philosophy and rhetoric.

While it became accepted for these educated women to engage in the political thought and debate of the time, publishing letters, dialogues, and treatises, their participation in this learned culture appears to have been very much limited to young, single women. It was almost a pastime for them to engage in before their "proper" jobs as wives and mothers began. Even though a significant number of humanist women have been identified from the quattrocento, almost every single one put down the pen once she was married; one study of more than thirty such women writers shows that only one continued her work after she married, though another restarted her intellectual pursuits when she was widowed.[39]

Women humanists were extolled for their virtue and intellect but in a way that made them mere adornments to the crowns of the men around them. Plenty of male humanists wrote exaggerated compliments to and about these women, but their praise always came at the cost of other women, or as a way to extol their society at large, rather than simply complimenting women for their own sake. Ludovico Maria Sforza, later Duke of Milan, wrote in 1490, "Fortunate is your father, who chanced to procreate a daughter blessed with such gifts of mind and nature. Happiest is the city of Venice, which has obtained in its citizen Cassandra [Fedele] an ornament for the greatness of its empire and heroic deeds, because nature wanted to test in her what was possible in the female sex."[40]

Cassandra Fedele, one of the most famous female humanist writers of Italy, received similar "praise" from the scholar and poet Angelo Poliziano, when he wrote to her: "In our age, in which it is rare for even men to excel in letters, you are the only maiden living who handles a book instead of wool, a reed pen instead of make-up, a metal stilus instead of a needle, and who smears not her skin with white lead, but rather paper with ink. This indeed is as extraordinary, as rare, as new, as if violets took root amid ice, roses in snow, or lilies in ice."[41] Angelo held Cassandra aloft of all other women for her mind, more like a man's than a woman's, for instead of involving herself with what he considered frivolous female vices, she was dedicated to her studies.

But just as Italian men could glorify women for their knowledge, they could also viciously destroy them if they were perceived to

This manuscript miniature from Ovid's *Heroides* (*Heroines*) captures a noblewoman writing.

Robinet Testard (active c. 1471–1531)
Ovid, *Heroides* (detail), fol. 1r, France, 1497
Bibliothèque Nationale de France, Paris;
Français 875

step out of line. Isotta Nogarola lived in the first half of the fifteenth century and is considered by many to have been the first
major female humanist. Despite this modern accolade, at the time
she was essentially a lone woman trying to break into the world of
men. Because she had dared to try to engage in written and spoken
debates with men, a cruel campaign was launched against her. A
published pamphlet accused her of being a prostitute and of having
an incestuous relationship with her brother. After the release of this
diatribe, she left the city of Venice and moved in with her mother
to live a less public life.[42]

The dislike of women's participation in what many men wished
to regard as their domain, alongside the idea that a woman's brains
could not attain the same heights as a man's, meant that many
women writers of the Middle Ages had to constantly defend themselves against accusations that they were not the true authors of
their texts. Laura Cereta of Brescia in northern Italy was given an
exemplary education by her father and began publishing Latin letters and orations when she was around twenty years old, but she
soon had to write letters defending herself as the true author of the
works because of the disbelief of her male contemporaries. Even
Christine de Pisan, such an established and much-commissioned
author, was not safe from such accusations. In 1475, a presumably
male translator from Bruges added a note to his translation of her
City of Ladies in which he questioned how such an excellent work
could possibly have been written by a woman; instead, he suggested
it must have had a male author who wished to write anonymously.[43]
Women could therefore participate in the written culture of the
Middle Ages—but they would expect to be vilified for doing so.

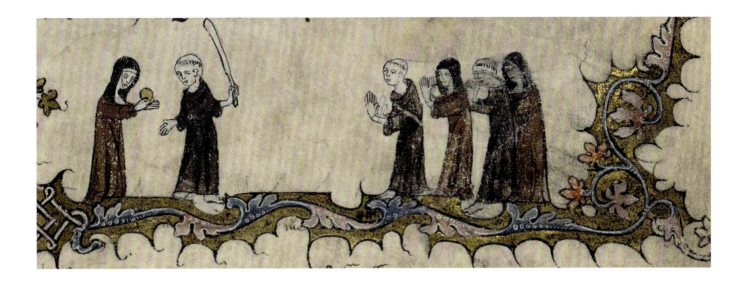

MANUSCRIPT PRODUCTION

With an explosion in the written word, writers needed something to hold their many texts. Creating manuscripts in the Middle Ages was an incredibly labor-intensive process, slowly made easier by advances in technology. Up until the very end of the medieval period, all European books were written by hand. Scribes would assiduously copy out texts, a process that could take months or even years, depending on their skill, the size of the text, and the stature of the project.

But writing was not the only consideration in creating manuscripts. Books were expensive, prestigious objects because of the time and care it took to make them, and their owners wanted them to be beautiful. Many manuscripts were therefore intricately ornamented with border patterns, decorated initials, and accompanying miniatures painted in a plethora of expensive pigments. Writing and decorating manuscripts was usually undertaken by multiple people to speed up the process. Books were bound together only when the product was finished, leaving loose sheets that could be passed around concurrently, so that one page was being decorated while the next was being written. The production of manuscripts thus required careful collaboration between writer and artist.

Earlier in the medieval period, a significant proportion of people creating and copying texts were residents of religious houses, as they were the ones with the skills, education, and resources to do so. As the period progressed and books became more widespread, monks and nuns continued this work but were increasingly joined by secular scribes. Scribes differed from writers in that they copied out texts rather than created original works, but this does not make their work any less important—and indeed, some scribes also picked up the pen as writers. In a time when the skill of writing was not widespread, women who engaged in scribal work were making important contributions to society.

We have seen how vital the involvement of nuns was to the written word across the medieval period, like Hildegard of Bingen, who we met earlier. Generally, their work was revered, and their writing

Hildegard of Bingen was a famous medieval mystic known across Europe. This is one image from *Scivias*, a text she wrote describing her visions, which was originally read to the pope to confirm her authenticity. Although it seems unlikely that Hildegard herself illustrated her manuscript, she almost certainly had strong oversight over the images and probably directed the artist. Sadly, Hildegard's original manuscript of c. 1175 was lost during the Second World War, but in 1933 it had been faithfully copied by a group of nuns at the Benedictine Abbey of Saint Hildegard.

Nuns of the Benedictine Abbey of Saint Hildegard
Hildegard of Bingen, *Scivias*, Germany, 1933
Benediktinerinnenabtei Sankt Hildegard, Eibingen, Germany

Nuns who wrote and decorated manuscripts sometimes placed self-portraits inside. Drawn by Guda, a German nun, this image is one of the first signed self-portraits of a Western woman.

Guda (12th century)
Homiliary of Guda, fol. 110v, Germany, 1150–1200
Frankfurt am Main Universitatsbibliothek, Germany; Ms. Barth. 42

often specifically sought out. For example, in the twelfth century, Idung of Prüfening wrote *A Dialogue between Two Monks*, addressing the preface to Kunigunde, abbess of Niedermünster, in Germany, and requesting that the nuns of the monastery make a copy of this work and that they correct it along the way.[44] But others were suspicious of bringing women—particularly religious women—into this process, especially when it would mean interacting with men. In joint monasteries, or in female houses where male scribes also practiced, nuns working in a scriptorium risked breaking careful segregation. One friar writing in the thirteenth century highlighted this uncomfortable reality and sought to limit women's participation; he wrote that while female scribes could sit in the communal room with male writers, they "should not write other things as long as the convent has the necessary books."[45] As we have seen, parts of society held to the belief that women needed only a limited exposure to the written word, and they should not be involved in its reading or its production any more than was essential.

These scribe-nuns were highly skilled at their work. Literate nuns would have taken dictation from their fellow sisters or brothers, a difficult task that required carefully listening and quickly noting down words using cumbersome tools like ink and quills or wax tablets and styluses. As we saw with Idung's text, these scribes were also often expected to make corrections and improve comprehension when they wrote out their notes into finished pieces. Irimbert, a twelfth-century monk at the joint monastery of Admont, in Austria, records with praise the work of the scribal nuns there. At one point, two nuns were assigned to transcribe his teachings full-time, and in the 1140s as many as eleven nuns helped him to copy and edit some of his religious commentaries.[46]

While many nuns wrote as part of their daily lives, certain events could encourage their increased participation in the craft. This largely centered around religious reform, which was spurred through several events. Over time, some religious institutions collectively decided that the order they followed no longer suited them, and they decided to change to a different rule. A monastery could gain a new abbess who was particularly zealous and wanted to shape up things within her house. Or reform could come as part of a wider movement across an order, region, or Europe as a whole, as with the so-called Observant Reform, which started in the fourteenth century and focused on a return to the original, correct observance of monastic rules.[47] Whatever the reason, whether the new order engaged with different texts or the old texts were considered outdated or incorrect, religious reform and revival often led to an immediate need for many new books. While outside commissions could be sought, it made economic sense to task the house's own nuns with some of the production of these texts.

Female religious institutions across Europe were home to thousands of books. More than 4,000 manuscripts from women's convents survive from late medieval Germany; and of 1,250 extant Middle Dutch manuscripts from religious communities in the Low Countries, 75 percent came from female institutions, and most of those were written by nuns.[48] It is no surprise to find, then, that religious women took on such a key role in manuscript production, though they are much more commonly depicted in art as readers of books than writers.

Nuns who wrote were also quick to pick up technological innovations in their craft. The European printing press was invented by Johannes Gutenberg in Germany around 1440, and within a few decades, the technology had begun to spread across the continent. This machine allowed for mass production of texts by pressing ink onto paper with metal type pieces. This meant thousands of pages could be printed in one day from a single press, as opposed to a handful of pages written by hand. Nuns were quick to pool their resources and use their contacts to purchase these new machines and thus were on the forefront of innovation.

The women of the convent of Corpus Domini in Bologna made use of the town's first printing press in 1470 to publish a copy of *Sette armi spirituali* (*Seven Spiritual Weapons*). This had been composed earlier in the century by one of their sisters, Catherine de Vigri, who was revered in the surrounding area and later made a saint. This printed copy went on to become a best seller and boosted Catherine's reputation and that of her nunnery. Elsewhere in Italy, the convent of San Jacopo di Ripoli in Florence bought one of the first printing presses in Italy in the 1470s. The nuns used donations from a laywoman, a loan from their prioress, and a gift from one of their sisters to buy the type matrices, and they quickly turned their convent into a mass printing hub. They sold thousands of copies

of saints' lives and other religious texts such as psalms, which they printed in both Latin and the vernacular.[49]

Sometimes, though, innovation was a lot simpler. Toward the end of the Middle Ages, the concept of a table of contents was slowly introduced. Women who had heard of this new addition to some manuscripts were quick to try it for themselves. The nun Anna Eybin, made provost of her convent at Pillenreuth, Germany, in 1461, was enthusiastic in obtaining books for her sisters, and she actively compiled, copied, and wrote many books for her community. One of her surviving manuscripts, written between 1465 and 1485, was a compilation of saints' lives, biblical stories, and sermons. As it was over two hundred pages long, Anna decided to implement a table of contents to help her readers navigate to the texts.

Anna was no expert, however, and her use of the contents is somewhat inconsistent. Medieval contents were initially much more descriptive than ours today—they did not simply name the chapter and provide its page number but instead included summaries of texts. Anna's contents run for eleven pages but miss the last four texts as it appears she ran out of her allotted space. She explains to her readers how a table of contents works—showing that the concept was new and unfamiliar—but then does not give page numbers for some of the texts. Meanwhile, she provides just a line or two in summary for some parts, while others receive far more, like the "Life of Queen Anastasia," a ten-page story for which she provides three pages of summary. Though the table of contents of Anna's manuscript is messy, it gives us a fantastic opportunity to watch a medieval female writer practice a new system.[50]

Once a medieval text had been created, it often needed to be decorated. Inside the scriptorium of a monastery, this could be done in-house by fellow monks or nuns, and because of the skill required, the artist usually would be a different person from the scribe. If a convent could not afford art supplies, then the sisters might turn to their outside relatives for help. As they could not have money of their own, using their connections was often the only way they could obtain the expensive brushes and pigments.[51] The decoration of manuscripts is a great way to find medieval women artists, as they often used the opportunity to name or portray themselves.

$\mathfrak{S}$ ib esille 7 entotrue
$\mathfrak{L}$ fir illes toit procurer
$\mathfrak{T}$ bicn qnil lour toic diuer
$\mathfrak{Y}$ aier friill alui facorte
$\mathfrak{W}$ fouge tottetitor: lacorte
$\mathfrak{W}$ le fet henner 7 retitre

$\mathfrak{Y}$ onr aur qimidn prmit
$\mathfrak{N}$ estoit il nens qtoit trint
$\mathfrak{H}$ onqs pms nens ne me prattes
$\mathfrak{S}$ eslore q patnois amattes
$\mathfrak{W}$ mar nc me toulet prtier
$\mathfrak{A}$ nr fcffoirent dapriacr

These two sets of portraits show the illuminator couple Jeanne and Richard de Montbaston, who were well known in Paris for their artistic skills. Jeanne continued her work after Richard died, and her contribution was almost lost to history. These little portraits remind us of her presence—and of that of other female artists.

Jeanne de Montbaston (active c. 1320s–1355); Richard de Montbaston (active c. 1320s–1353)
Guillaume de Lorris and Jean de Meun, *Le Roman de la rose* (details), fols. 77r and 77v, France, 14th century
Bibliothèque Nationale de France, Paris; Français 25526

Plenty of nuns' self-portraits can be found in the margins—or even centers—of the books they produced throughout the centuries: Maria Ormani in a 1453 breviary, as we saw earlier; a German nun named Guda in her twelfth-century homilies; an unknown woman in a thirteenth-century medical manuscript—the list goes on.[52] These images are a fantastic connection to the women who created them centuries ago.

Though it is easier for us to identify nuns who produced manuscripts, secular women became involved as the process developed. Sometimes we know about them only from passing references; Christine de Pisan mentions a female painter she knew named Anastaise, who was "so skillful and experienced in painting borders and miniatures of manuscripts that no one can cite an artist in the city of Paris . . . who in these endeavors surpasses her."[53] This Anastaise has never been further identified, but she clearly made a significant mark in her time.

As with other secular professions, many women involved in making manuscripts were drawn in as part of a family business. There are multiple instances of women working with their fathers or husbands to produce artwork, and Paris was certainly the hub of this in Europe. As decorating large manuscripts was often a group task, these women could be commissioned alongside the men in their family to produce significant pieces of art for the highest echelons of society. Bourgot de Noir, for instance, was active around the 1350s, working alongside her father, Jehan, to fulfill commissions from the French court.[54]

One well-known illuminator couple was Richard and Jeanne de Montbaston, who worked in Paris from the 1320s to the 1350s. They have been identified both in the official record and by clues they left in the manuscripts they produced. In 1348, Richard very openly recorded his name and address in a manuscript that he decorated as an advertisement for future work. Richard had painted 140 miniatures in the manuscript by himself, but on many manuscripts, Jeanne and Richard worked together—and it has been discovered that Jeanne also illuminated some manuscripts by herself. While Richard appears to have been professionally trained in his art, as his figures show greater skill, Jeanne's work is by no means poor, and

she demonstrates her own style in her drawings, such as those for Arthurian romances.

Historians have identified at least fifty manuscripts that Richard and Jeanne worked on, and almost all of them were written in the vernacular. They also appear to have become renowned for their illustration of *Le Roman de la rose*, a French poem on the theme of romantic love, for nineteen of the fifty manuscripts were copies of the *Roman*. Many of these were illuminated either by Richard or Jeanne, but they decorated a few together.[55] Because such manuscripts were commissioned by patrons, each edition was illustrated differently— the patrons would choose how many pictures they wanted, what they wanted the pictures to show, and their sizes and placement in the manuscript, depending on their budget.

While some manuscripts did have particularly large pictures that corresponded with the narrative, the marginalia that decorated the edges of the page were largely added at the discretion of the artist and very often did not correspond to the text. This meant that illiterate artists could decorate manuscripts, for they did not need to understand the writing; they could discuss the designs of particular images with their patrons, making notes on placement and style on the page to guide them when it came time to decorate, with other parts left to their discretion. This was certainly the case for Jeanne, who seems to have been illiterate or to have had very little ability to read. Whereas Richard left small marginal notes to himself, which would become hidden once the book was bound, Jeanne made sketches that she could refer to and paint over when completing the images.[56]

Jeanne and Richard were engaged with secular, vernacular manuscripts, and this meant that their work did not need to be of the highest quality, since many patrons wanted the illustrations completed quickly and cheaply. The content of the drawings matched the courtly, often irreverent tone of the manuscripts—these were no holy tomes, and the couple decorated the margins with bawdy images that would have entertained their readers. This does not mean, though, that their skills were unappreciated; both Jeanne and Richard were employed by French nobles and royals. Jeanne illuminated a philosophical book that has a frontispiece of the

↑ The illuminator Jeanne de Montbaston was a skilled artist and used gold leaf and expensive inks to bring her characters to life. This miniature shows a scene from an Arthurian romance of Tristan speaking to King Arthur, Queen Genevieve, and other knights.

Jeanne de Montbaston (active c. 1320s–1355)
Roman du Bon Chevalier Tristan . . . , fol. 337v, France (Paris), 1320–40
Getty, Los Angeles; Ms. Ludwig XV 5

↗ Jeanne de Montbaston brought her figures to life with exciting movement that often went outside the frames she had drawn, as in this picture of Arthurian knight Tristan freeing a damsel.

Jeanne de Montbaston (active c. 1320s–1355)
Roman du Bon Chevalier Tristan . . . , fol. 260r, France (Paris), 1320–40
Getty, Los Angeles; Ms. Ludwig XV 5

arms of France and Navarre, leading to the suggestion it was made for Jeanne of France, queen of Navarre. She also likely decorated a custom-made anthology that was gifted to the French king as he was preparing for a crusade.[57]

Jeanne de Montbaston demonstrates how highly regarded a skilled woman could be for her craft, but she also shows just how easy it is for us to miss the presence of women among creators of art. The only reason we know her true identity is because Richard predeceased her. Illuminators in Paris were required to take an official oath with the university to practice their trade, which Richard had taken in 1338. Working as Richard's wife, Jeanne had not needed to take it herself, but after Richard died, she was required to take the oath as an independent woman artist. She swore this oath in July 1353, and that is how we know her name.[58] If she had died first, then her identity may well have been lost to us.

Jeanne and Richard left us tantalizing joint self-portraits in the margins of one of their many copies of the *Roman de la rose*, where the couple is shown on both sides of a page. On one side, Jeanne sits grinding pigment into colors while Richard writes on a piece of calfskin. On the other side, Jeanne paints initial decorations on a page while Richard draws their outlines, and finished pages hang drying behind them. Even if we had lost Jeanne's name, her presence was still visible in the margins. This situation was by no means unique, for a few decades before the Montbastons, another Parisian couple had been in the same situation. Jean de Laigny and his wife, Ameline de Berron, illuminated manuscripts together in the latter half of the thirteenth century. When Jean died in 1298, Ameline

succeeded him as a solo artist.[59] Many female manuscript artists can be considered to have been lost to the records, then, and as with other professions, we must continue to assume that a portion of unidentified artists were indeed women.

Art and writing were at the heart of medieval culture, and women could be found participating at all levels. From the peasants who created textiles to decorate their homes, to the professionals who earned a living by painting and copying books, to the noblewomen who crafted skillful pieces out of the most luxurious materials or patronized other women creators, women left a significant cultural impact across Europe. Being a nun, in particular, was an instrumental way that women could contribute to the arts—nuns copied texts and composed their own pieces, decorated manuscripts, created garments and decorations for their churches, and were often at the forefront of innovation.

Women knew how to manipulate art for their own needs and recognized the political worth that could come from these pieces beyond their beauty. They created and ordered texts and textiles that would glorify their families and prop up the women around them, using the written word to argue for the participation of women in all parts of society. Many women found their way into the arts through virtue of their families, but this made them no less respected than their male counterparts. Though men would scoff at women's education, doubting their skills and legitimacy, women continued to push for their right to read, write, and create.

↖ Though their work often went unsigned, many women participated in the arts, from illustrating manuscripts to painting the walls of churches. In this manuscript illumination from a French translation of Boccaccio's *De claris mulieribus* (*Concerning Famous Women*), a woman draws an outline for a fresco onto a wall.

Robinet Testard (active c. 1471–1531)
Giovanni Boccaccio, *Des cleres et nobles femmes*, fol. 53v, France, 1488–96
Bibliothèque Nationale de France;
Français 599

↑ A seated woman carefully paints a statue of the Virgin Mary and infant Jesus.

Giovanni Boccaccio, *Des cleres et nobles femmes*, fol. 92v, France, 1401–1500
Bibliothèque Nationale de France, Paris; Français 12420

THE LEGACY OF WOMEN IN ART

Women played vital roles in the Middle Ages. All across Europe they were at the heart of everyday life. They toiled in the fields, cared for children in the home, crafted intricately beautiful pieces of art, wrote intensely intelligent treatises, and led troops into battle. Far from the vision of the quiet, subservient woman who did nothing but give birth, medieval women had dynamic lives, and were very much involved in society.

When records are silent, then the vibrant art created in this period can speak. Countless peasants whose names are lost to history come to life sprawled across the margins of manuscripts. Craftswomen left their mark stitch by stitch, paint stroke by paint stroke, and their exquisite creations have lasted for centuries or even a millennium, long after they were forgotten. Women shaped art, but they were also shaped by it; they took inspiration from the visions of women that they saw around them. As the Virgin Mary read in stained glass windows of their churches, so too did they learn to read.

What may be surprising to us is just how many options a medieval woman had open to her. Far from being pigeonholed into the role of wife or nun, women had nuanced choices. While some cultures might have higher expectations of marriage and motherhood, other parts of Europe were more open to allowing young women freedom to explore before settling down. These maidens could travel to towns, learn a trade, and set up a business, building their own independent wealth and reputation. Their skills were no less admired than those of the men around them, and they would be specially sought to produce objects for patrons. Writers would sing their praises, but this could come at the cost of disparaging other women, and creative women found themselves followed by suspicion that their talents could not possibly be their own but instead those of a man hiding his identity.

If a woman chose to dedicate herself to the church, she eventually found that even there she had far more possibilities than women in previous centuries. Life in a strictly cloistered convent, while appealing to some, was not the only way a woman could get closer to God. She could live in a chaste community of beguines or vowesses, dwelling in sisterhood away from the overbearing presence of men while having a simple life in which she could find personal pleasure and salvation. This option was open to women at any stage of life, so that even dying widows could find a way to ease their pathway into heaven.

Bayeux Tapestry, England, c. 1070
Detail of page 157

183

→ The most recognizable woman in European art was the Virgin Mary, mother of Jesus. Mary was the idealized woman, and medieval women were expected to emulate her in their own lives. Images of Mary adorned homes, churches, buildings, and household objects as a permanent reminder of her holiness and her key role in the salvation of humanity.

Fra Angelico (c. 1400–1455)
Madonna of Humility, Italy (Florence), c. 1440
Tempera on panel, 29⅛ × 20½ in. (74 × 52 cm)
Rijksmuseum, Amsterdam

↓ Although peasant women were often depicted working, they did not always live hand-to-mouth, and they did find time to socialize. This charming base panel of a manuscript page shows shepherdesses and shepherds dancing among their sheep, while one person plays a bagpipe.

Book of hours, fol. 56r, France (Rouen), c. 1400 -90
Walters Art Museum, Baltimore; W.225

Joining the church was an important way that a medieval woman could exert autonomy over her life. Instead of having a husband and a future chosen for her, she could select which order and institution she entered. If she had power and money, she could even found a convent of her own. While male members of the church would keep an eye on how the institution was run, these female communities could often live largely outside of male rule—as women led by women. The church not only opened spiritual opportunities, but convents provided many ways for a woman to develop herself that she might have been denied in the secular world. Here, she had time and resources to become educated, learning to read, write, paint, or sew. For women of the lower classes, this was an invaluable opportunity.

Noblewomen sat at the pinnacle of society. Through the luck of their birth, they had a seat at the table of power. Though they were almost always expected to marry for the political gain of their family, they found great power through these unions. They married landowners and rulers and shared responsibilities with their husbands. They managed households and estates, cared for servants and tenants, and entertained courtiers. They wrote letters, influenced policies, and pleaded for mercy for those who found themselves the subject of a leader's wrath. In some cases, they even discovered that they could inspire armies to follow them, defending their rights against the men who would try to remove them.

The Middle Ages saw a massive change in society. From smaller, disparate territories of individual cultures and numerous religions grew cohesive nation-states and kingdoms largely joined under

↖ Even women's personal, everyday items like combs were decorated with art. One side of this ivory comb shows an older couple entering the Fountain of Youth and coming out as a young woman and man. Though the comb was used for beauty reasons, this scene is actually satirical because it shows a fool sitting by the fountain, highlighting the couple's folly for looking for eternal youth. The other side features a hunting scene.

Comb, Upper Rhine or Burgundy, 15th century
Carved ivory, 5⅝ × 5¾ in. (14.5 × 14.7 cm)
Victoria and Albert Museum, London

↑ This embroidered purse showcases a woman holding a dog while a man offers her a flower or a ring.

Purse, France, early 14th century
Silk, linen, and gold leaf, 5½ × 6 in.
(14 × 15.2 cm)
Metropolitan Museum of Art, New York

Iaia of Cyzicus was a famous ancient Greek painter whose reputation continued into the medieval period. This image of Iaia using a handheld mirror to complete a self-portrait decorated a translation of Boccaccio's *De claris mulieribus* (*Concerning Famous Women*), which provided role models for medieval women.

Giovanni Boccaccio, *Des cleres et nobles femmes*, fol. 101v, France, 1401–1500
Bibliothèque Nationale de France, Paris; Français 12420

Christendom. Cultures, goods, and information were shared between territories aided by a growth in population and technology. As the world expanded, so too did women's opportunities, but progress was not a straight line, and women's rights fluctuated. As society developed, women sometimes found themselves pushed to the margins by the men around them who wanted to take the spoils for their own. But their legacy has remained in the art created by them and about them. Through this, we can gain insight into these women who lived centuries ago.

ACKNOWLEDGMENTS

This book has been such a pleasure to work on, and there are many people whom I would like to thank for making it so. Firstly, the wonderful Danièle Cybulskie, who has not just been a supporter of my writing from the very start, but who put me in touch with Abbeville Press to write this book. To my editor, Lauren Orthey, for giving me the opportunity to pull this all together—it was fantastic to find an editor who had the same vision for the book as I did (and who let me stretch my definition of the due date). Also to Amy Hughes for her assiduous copy editing. A thank-you too to all the staff at the British Library who persevered through a cyberattack to make as much of their collection available for consultation as possible. Without their work, I would have struggled to find such a variety of voices from across Europe to compile. I must mention too all the kind and supportive historians with whom I have made friends on Twitter/X over the years. David Veevers, Danie Burton, Sharon Bennett Connolly, Amy Boucher, Sylvia Barbara Soberton, Matthew Lewis, and many others whose names I can't fit in here, have been invaluable across my career as an author. They really give historians a good name, and have done so much to help me and have inspired me to be a better researcher and writer. For all the faults of social media, the willingness of the historical community to share research and good reviews is a big marker in its favor.

Finally, a few more personal thank-yous. To my Mum, Claudia, and Glyn for once more stepping up to be my proofreaders when my words were just a pile of mush on a page. I (and my readers) thank you for catching my mistakes and for encouraging my ideas. To my work colleagues who gave me leniency to spend time writing and researching. To Nick Connell, for still being a bouncing board for our respective projects and someone to (lovingly) complain about writing to. To Tess, for always willingly being on hand to provide me with suggested readings. To my friends who distracted me from writing when I needed it and sent encouraging messages when it felt like it would never get done—Harriet, Ella, Camilla, Lianne, Pam, Florence, Aurora, and Rhianna. And to Conor, for dealing with me becoming a hermit in my study, for helping me plot through ideas and case studies, and for nagging me to sit down and write instead of cleaning the house for the fifth time. I hope you can place this beautiful book on your shelves knowing that you all helped make it happen.

NOTES

I. PEASANTS AND PROFESSIONALS

1   Jane Whittle, "Housewives and Servants in Rural England, 1440–1650: Evidence of Women's Work from Probate Documents," *Transactions of the Royal Historical Society* 15 (2005): 63; *The Ballad of the Tyrannical Husband*, trans. Jeremy Goldberg, 2002, University of York, https://www.york.ac.uk/teaching/history/pjpg/BALLAD.htm.

2   Mercedes Borrero Fernández, "Peasant and Aristocratic Women: Their Role and the Rural Economy of Seville at the End of the Middle Ages," in *Women at Work in Spain: From the Middle Ages to Early Modern Times*, eds. Marilyn Stone and Carmen Benito-Vessels (New York: Peter Lang, 1998), 13–20.

3   D. J. Stone, "The Consumption of Field Crops in Late Medieval England," in *Food in Medieval England: Diet and Nutrition*, eds. C. M. Woolgar, D. Serjeantson, and T. Waldron (Oxford: Oxford University Press, 2006), 15–18; Whittle, "Housewives and Servants," 71.

4   Constance Hoffman Berman, *The White Nuns: Cistercian Abbeys for Women in Medieval France* (Philadelphia: University of Pennsylvania Press, 2018), 36; David Herlihy, *Opera Muliebria: Women and Work in Medieval Europe* (New York and London: McGraw-Hill, 1990), 64; Steinunn Kristjánsdóttir, "The Abbesses of Iceland," *Religions* 14, no. 4 (2023): article 533, 10.

5   Christopher Dyer, "The Material World of English Peasants, 1200–1540: Archaeological Perspectives on Rural Economy and Welfare," *Agricultural History Review* 62, no. 1 (2014): 2–7.

6   Ibid., 13.

7   As quoted in Herlihy, *Opera Muliebria*, 76–78.

8   Jeffrey F. Hamburger, *Nuns as Artists: The Visual Culture of a Medieval Convent* (Berkeley: University of California Press, 1997), 186–87.

9   Shelley E. Roff, "'Appropriate to Her Sex?' Women's Participation on the Construction Site in Medieval and Early Modern Europe," in *Women and Wealth in Late Medieval Europe*, ed. Theresa Earenfight (New York: Palgrave Macmillan, 2010), 112; Herlihy, *Opera Muliebria*, 60, 167; Martha C. Howell, *Women, Production, and Patriarchy in Late Medieval Cities* (Chicago: University of Chicago Press, 1986), 16.

10 Sharon Farmer, "Merchant Women and the Administrative Glass Ceiling in Thirteenth-Century Paris," in *Women and Wealth in Late Medieval Europe*, ed. Theresa Earenfight (New York: Palgrave Macmillan, 2010), 89; R. H. Britnell, "Specialization of Work in England, 1100–1300," *Economic History Review* 54, no. 1 (2001): 1; Roff, "'Appropriate to Her Sex?,'" 112.

11 Roff, "'Appropriate to Her Sex?,'" 110, 117.

12 James M. Murray, *Bruges, Cradle of Capitalism, 1280–1390* (Cambridge: Cambridge University Press, 2005), 307; Jeremy Goldberg, *Women, Work, and Life Cycle in a Medieval Economy: Women in York and Yorkshire c. 1300–1520* (Oxford: Clarendon Press, 1992), 104–5.

13 Justin Colson, "A Portrait of a Late Medieval London Pub: The Star Inn, Bridge Street," in *Medieval Londoners: Essays to Mark the Eightieth Birthday of Caroline M. Barron*, eds. Elizabeth A. New and Christian Steer (London: University of London Press, 2019), 38–44; Murray, *Bruges*, 318–19.

14 Barbara A. Hanawalt, "Medieval English Women in Rural and Urban Domestic Space," *Dumbarton Oaks Papers* 52 (1998): 24–26.

15 Goldberg, *Women, Work*, 152; Kim M. Phillips, *Medieval Maidens: Young Women and Gender in England, 1270–1540* (Manchester, UK: Manchester University Press, 2003), 132; Herlihy, *Opera Muliebria*, 155–58.

16 Murray, *Bruges*, 328, 342.

17 Ibid., 339–42.

18 Ruth Mazo Karras, "The Regulation of Brothels in Later Medieval England," in "Working Together in the Middle Ages: Perspectives on Women's Communities," *Signs: Journal of Women in Culture and Society* 14, no. 2 (1989): 107.

19 Goldberg, *Women, Work*, 152–54.

20 Hanawalt, "Medieval English Women," 23; Murray, *Bruges*, 327.

21 Phillips, *Medieval Maidens*, 113–16; Whittle, "Housewives and Servants," 61–62.

22 Whittle, "Housewives and Servants," 54–66.

23 Phillips, *Medieval Maidens*, 110, 128.

24 Roff, "'Appropriate to Her Sex?,'" 116.

25 Farmer, "Merchant Women," 93, 101.

26 Herlihy, *Opera Muliebria*, 69–70, 94–96.

27 Farmer, "Merchant Women," 93–95.

28 Herlihy, *Opera Muliebria*, 84–91.

29 Emily A. Holmes, *Flesh Made Word: Medieval Women Mystics, Writing, and the Incarnation* (Waco, TX: Baylor University Press, 2013), 50; Herlihy, *Opera Muliebria*, 69–70.

30 Maryanne Kowaleski and Judith M. Bennett, "Crafts, Gilds, and Women in the Middle Ages: Fifty Years after Marian K. Dale," in "Working Together in the Middle Ages: Perspectives on Women's Communities," *Signs: Journal of Women in Culture and Society* 14, no. 2 (1989): 474–501.

31 Murray, *Bruges*, 308; Howell, *Women, Production, and Patriarchy*, 49.

32 Howell, *Women, Production, and Patriarchy*, 62.

33 Herlihy, *Opera Muliebria*, 94–95.

34 Goldberg, *Women, Work*, 143; Whittle, "Housewives and Servants," 71.

35 Goldberg, *Women, Work*, 127–28.

36 Herlihy, *Opera Muliebria*, 168–69.

37 Meredith Parsons Lillich, "Gothic Glaziers: Monks, Jews, Taxpayers, Bretons, Women," *Journal of Glass Studies* 27 (1985): 72–92.

38 Roff, "'Appropriate to Her Sex?,'" 114.

39 Ibid., 115, 119.

40 Eileen Power (trans.), *The Goodman of Paris (Le Ménagier de Paris): A Treatise on Moral and Domestic Economy by a Citizen of Paris, c. 1393* (Woodbridge, UK: Boydell Press, 2006), 173, 192–94.

41 Montserrat Cabré, "Women or Healers? Household Practices and the Categories of Health Care in Late Medieval Iberia," in "Women, Health, and Healing in Early Modern Europe," special issue, *Bulletin of the History of Medicine* 82, no. 1 (2008): 40.

42 Montserrat Cabré, "From a Master to a Laywoman: A Feminine Manual of Self-Help," *Dynamis: Acta Hispanica ad Medicinae Scientiarumque Historiam Illustrandam* 20 (2000): 377.

43 Herlihy, *Opera Muliebria*, 104–5, 110.

44 Ibid., 107–9.

45 Monica Green, "Women's Medical Practice and Health Care in Medieval Europe," in "Working Together in the Middle Ages: Perspectives on Women's Communities," *Signs: Journal of Women in Culture and Society* 14, no. 2 (1989): 447–48.

46 Ibid., 448.

47 Cabré, "Women or Healers?," 24; Green, "Women's Medical Practice," 454–55.

48 Herlihy, *Opera Muliebria*, 107, 173; Green, "Women's Medical Practice," 443–44.

49 Caley McCarthy, "The Valuation of Care Work: Wet Nurses at the Hôpital du Saint-Esprit in Marseille," in "Gender and the History of Care Work," *Clio: Women, Gender, History*, no. 49 (2019): 48, 57, 60.

50 Ibid., 56.

51 Ibid., 50–51.

52 Ibid., 55.

II. RELIGIOUS WOMEN

1 Leonard P. Hindsley, *The Mystics of Engelthal: Writings from a Medieval Monastery* (New York: St. Martin's Press, 1998), 3.
2 Constance Hoffman Berman, *The White Nuns: Cistercian Abbeys for Women in Medieval France* (Philadelphia: University of Pennsylvania Press, 2018), ix.
3 Tracy Collins, "Space and Place: Archaeologies of Female Monasticism in Later Medieval Ireland," in *Gender in Medieval Places, Spaces and Thresholds*, eds. Victoria Blud, Diane Heath, and Einat Klafter (London: University of London Press, 2019), 27; Henrietta Leyser, *Medieval Women: A Social History of Women in England 450–1500* (London: Phoenix Press, 2002), 190.
4 Hindsley, *The Mystics of Engelthal*, xiii, xxi.
5 Ibid., 5; Karen Stöber, "Female Patrons of Late Medieval English Monasteries," *Medieval Prosopography* 31 (2016): 124; Katherine Clark, "Purgatory, Punishment, and the Discourse of Holy Widowhood in the High and Later Middle Ages," *Journal of the History of Sexuality* 16, no. 2 (2007): 169–203.
6 Henrietta Leyser, "Christina of Markyate: The Introduction," in *Christina of Markyate: A Twelfth-Century Holy Woman*, eds. Samuel Fanous and Henrietta Leyser (Oxford: Routledge, 2005), 1–5.
7 Leyser, *Medieval Women*, 214.
8 Thomas M. Izbicki, "Nuns' Clothing and Ornaments in English and Northern French Ecclesiastical Regulations," in *Refashioning Medieval and Early Modern Dress: A Tribute to Robin Netherton*, eds. Gale R. Owen-Crocker and Maren Clegg Hyer (Woodbridge, UK: Boydell and Brewer, 2019), 245.
9 Silvia Evangelisti, "'We Do Not Have It, and We Do Not Want It': Women, Power, and Convent Reform in Florence," *Sixteenth Century Journal* 34, no. 3 (2003): 693.
10 Penelope Johnson, *Equal in Monastic Profession: Religious Women in Medieval France* (Chicago: University of Chicago Press, 1991), 30–32; Berman, *The White Nuns*, 40.
11 Alison I. Beach, "Claustation and Collaboration between the Sexes in the Twelfth-Century Scriptorium," in *Monks and Nuns, Saints and Outcasts*, eds. Sharon Farmer and Barbara Rosenwein (Ithaca, NY, and London: Cornell University Press, 2000), 68–69.
12 Izbicki, "Nuns' Clothing," 248–49.
13 Luigi Pellegrini, "Female Religious Experience and Society in Thirteenth-Century Italy," in *Monks and Nuns, Saints and Outcasts*, eds. Sharon Farmer and Barbara Rosenwein (Ithaca, NY, and London: Cornell University Press, 2000), 105–7, 113–14.
14 Izbicki, "Nuns' Clothing," 237–54; Leyser, *Medieval Women*, 212.
15 Hindsley, *The Mystics of Engelthal*, 8–12.
16 David Herlihy, *Opera Muliebria: Women and Work in Medieval Europe* (New York and London: McGraw-Hill, 1990), 110.
17 Johnson, *Equal in Monastic Profession*, 50–54.
18 Leyser, *Medieval Women*, 206–7.
19 Steinunn Kristjánsdóttir, "The Abbesses of Iceland," *Religions* 14, no. 4 (2023): article 533, 3–4.
20 Herlihy, *Opera Muliebria*, 67–68.
21 Hindsley, *The Mystics of Engelthal*, xvii.
22 Clark, "Purgatory, Punishment," 188.
23 Beach, "Claustation and Collaboration," 60–61.
24 Mercedes Pérez Vidal, "The Corpus Christi Devotion: Gender, Liturgy, and Authority among Dominican Nuns in Castile in the Middle Ages," in "Gender and Status in the Medieval World," special issue, *Historical Reflections/ Réflexions Historiques* 42, no. 1 (2016): 37–40.
25 Evangelisti, "We Do Not Have It," 680; Leyser, *Medieval Women*, 190.
26 Collins, "Space and Place," 34–39; Berman, *The White Nuns*, xi, 26.
27 Hindsley, *The Mystics of Engelthal*, xxi.
28 Kristjánsdóttir, "The Abbesses of Iceland," 8; Johnson, *Equal in Monastic Profession*, 116–18.
29 Johnson, *Equal in Monastic Profession*, 128.
30 Sabina Flanagan, *Hildegard of Bingen: A Visionary Life* (London: Routledge, 1998), 1–7.
31 Hindsley, *The Mystics of Engelthal*, 14–15.
32 Rabia Gregory, "Thinking of Their Sisters: Authority and Authorship in Late Medieval Women's Religious Communities," *Journal of Medieval Religious Cultures* 40, no. 1 (2014): 76; Leyser, *Medieval Women*, 220.
33 Anne Llewellyn Barstow, "Joan of Arc and Female Mysticism," *Journal of Feminist Studies in Religion* 1, no. 2 (1985): 34.
34 Gregory, "Thinking of Their Sisters," 76; Hindsley, *The Mystics of Engelthal*, xxi.
35 Barstow, "Joan of Arc," 31–33.
36 Marilyn Oliva, "Counting Nuns: A Prosopography of Late Medieval English Nuns in the Diocese of Norwich," in "The Late Medieval English Church," special issue, *Medieval Prosopography* 16, no. 1 (1995): 27–55.
37 Johnson, *Equal in Monastic Profession*, 56.
38 Izbicki, "Nuns' Clothing," 242; Johnson, *Equal in Monastic Profession*, 55.
39 Karma Lochrie, *Heterosyncrasies: Female Sexuality When Normal Wasn't* (Minneapolis: University of Minnesota Press, 2005), 31.
40 Gemma Hollman, *Royal Witches: From Joan of Navarre to Elizabeth Woodville* (Cheltenham, UK: History Press, 2019), 264–67.

III. NOBLEWOMEN AND ROYALS

1 Geoffroy de La Tour-Landry, *The Book of the Knight of La Tour-Landry*, ed. Thomas Wright (London: Kegan Paul, Trench, Trubner, 1906), 18, 67.
2 Christine de Pisan, *The Treasure of the City of Ladies*, trans. Sarah Lawson (London: Penguin Books, 1985), 76.
3 Susan Schibanoff, "Botticelli's *Madonna del Magnificat*: Constructing the Woman Writer in Early Humanist Italy," *Publications of the Modern Language Association of America* 109, no. 2 (1994): 198–99.
4 Patricia-Ann Lee, "Reflections of Power: Margaret of Anjou and the Dark Side of Queenship," *Renaissance Quarterly* 39, no. 2 (1986): 196–97.
5 Richard Almond, "Femmes Fatale: Iconography and the Courtly Huntress in the Later Middle Ages and Renaissance," in *Deer and People*, eds. Karis Baker, Ruth Carden, and Richard Madgwick (Oxford: Oxbow Books, 2014), 257–63.
6 Kristin Juel, "Chess, Love, and the Rhetoric of Distraction in Medieval French Narrative," *Romance Philology* 64, no. 1 (2010): 73; Francesc de Castellví, Bernat Fenollar, and Narcís Vinyoles, *Scachs d'Amor*, trans. Josep Miquel Sobrer, n.d., https://www.scachsdamor.org/.
7 Paul Strohm, *Hochon's Arrow: The Social Imagination of Fourteenth-Century Texts* (Princeton, NJ: Princeton University Press, 1992), 95–96; Helen E. Maurer, *Margaret of Anjou: Queenship and Power in Late Medieval England* (Woodbridge, UK: Boydell Press, 2003), 11.
8 Gemma Hollman, *Royal Witches: From Joan of Navarre to Elizabeth Woodville* (Cheltenham, UK: History Press, 2019), 32.
9 David Baldwin, *Elizabeth Woodville: Mother of the Princes in the Tower* (Stroud, UK: Sutton, 2002), 10–11.
10 Henrietta Leyser, *Medieval Women: A Social History of Women in England 450–1500* (London: Phoenix Press, 2002), 107.
11 Aysu Dincer, "Wills, Marriage and Business Contracts: Urban Women in Late-Medieval Cyprus," *Gender and History* 24, no. 2 (2012): 315, 320.

12 Mark Ormrod, "The Royal Nursery: A Household for the Younger Children of Edward III," *English Historical Review* 120, no. 486 (2005): 398–415; Leyser, *Medieval Women*, 133–34.

13 Montserrat Piera, *Women Readers and Writers in Medieval Iberia: Spinning the Text* (Leiden, Netherlands, and Boston: Brill, 2019), 189–90.

14 Joanne M. Pierce, "'Green Women' and Blood Pollution: Some Medieval Rituals for the Churching of Women after Childbirth," *Studia Liturgica* 29, no. 2 (1999): 191–215; Caroline Shenton, "Philippa of Hainault's Churchings: The Politics of Motherhood at the Court of Edward III," in *Family and Dynasty: Proceedings of the 1997 Harlaxton Symposium*, Harlaxton Medieval Studies 9, ed. Richard Eales and Shaun Tyas (Donington, UK: Shaun Tyas, 2003), 106.

15 John Carmi Parsons, "The Pregnant Queen as Counsellor and the Medieval Construction of Motherhood," in *Medieval Mothering*, ed. John Carmi Parsons and Bonnie Wheeler (New York and London: Garland, 1996), 54.

16 Piera, *Women Readers*, 192.

17 Jacqueline Broad and Karen Green, *A History of Women's Political Thought in Europe, 1400–1700* (Cambridge: Cambridge University Press, 2009), 55–56.

18 Montserrat Cabré, "Women or Healers? Household Practices and the Categories of Health Care in Late Medieval Iberia," in "Women, Health, and Healing in Early Modern Europe," special issue, *Bulletin of the History of Medicine* 82, no. 1 (2008), 33.

19 John B. Freed, *Noble Bondsmen: Ministerial Marriages in the Archdiocese of Salzburg, 1100–1343* (Ithaca, NY, and London: Cornell University Press, 1995), 146.

20 Magna Carta, 1215, trans. British Library, National Archives, UK, https://www.nationalarchives.gov.uk/education/resources/magna-carta/british-library-magna-carta-1215-runnymede/.

21 Ffiona Swabey, *Medieval Gentlewoman: Life in a Widow's Household in the Later Middle Ages* (Stroud, UK: Sutton, 1999), 11; Susan Rose, *The Wine Trade in Medieval Europe 1000–1500* (London: Bloomsbury Academic, 2011), 113–23; John Stow, *Annals of England to 1603* (N.p.: c. 1603), 720.

22 "Although it is known that Queen Philippa does not have her right . . . ," Special Collections: Ancient Petitions; Petitions to the King . . . , SC 8/265/13210, National Archives, UK, https://discovery.nationalarchives.gov.uk/details/r/C9517157.

23 Mercedes Borrero Fernández, "Peasant and Aristocratic Women: Their Role and the Rural Economy of Seville at the End of the Middle Ages," in *Women at Work in Spain: From the Middle Ages to Early Modern Times*, eds. Marilyn Stone and Carmen Benito-Vessels (New York: Peter Lang, 1998), 23–24.

24 Karen Stöber, "Female Patrons of Late Medieval English Monasteries," *Medieval Prosopography* 31 (2016): 129–30.

25 Sara Cockerill, *Eleanor of Castile: The Shadow Queen* (Stroud, UK: Amberley, 2015), 15.

26 Piera, *Women Readers*, 217.

27 Roff, "'Appropriate to Her Sex?' Women's Participation on the Construction Site in Medieval and Early Modern Europe," 125; Veronica Sekules, "Dynasty and Patrimony in the Self-Construction of an English Queen: Philippa of Hainault and Her Images," in *England and the Continent in the Middle Ages: Proceedings of the 1996 Harlaxton Symposium*, Harlaxton Medieval Studies 8, ed. John Mitchell and Matthew Moran (Stamford, UK: Shaun Tyas, 2000), 168; Michael T. Davis, "A Gift from the Queen: The Architecture of the Collège de Navarre in Paris," in *Medieval Women and Their Objects*, eds. Jenny Adams and Nancy Mason Bradbury (Ann Arbor: University of Michigan Press, 2017), 71–76.

28 Ralph V. Turner, *Eleanor of Aquitaine: Queen of France, Queen of England* (New Haven, CT: Yale University Press, 2009), 115–16, 133–34, 175–76.

29 Hollman, *Royal Witches*, 91–94.

30 Charles Spencer, *The White Ship: Conquest, Anarchy and the Wrecking of Henry I's Dream* (London: Harper Collins, 2021).

31 Helen Castor, *She-Wolves: The Women Who Ruled England before Elizabeth* (London: Faber and Faber, 2011), 72–104.

32 Anna Brzezińska, "Jadwiga of Anjou as the Image of a Good Queen in Late Medieval and Early Modern Poland," *Polish Review* 44, no. 4 (1999): 407–18; Paul W. Knoll, "Jadwiga and Education," *Polish Review* 44, no. 4 (1999): 419–20.

33 Vivian Etting, *Queen Margrete I (1353–1412) and the Founding of the Nordic Union* (Leiden, Netherlands, and Boston: Brill, 2004), 96–100 and throughout.

34 *Oxford Dictionary of National Biography* (online), s.v. "Dunbar, Agnes, Countess of Dunbar and March," https://doi.org/10.1093/odnb/9780192683120.013.8200.

35 The marriage was not legal at the time for two reasons: first, Edward's father needed to grant permission for the marriage, and he had explicitly announced that he would not consent to the match; and second, Edward and his betrothed, Philippa, were within forbidden degrees of relation, and so they needed special permission from the pope to marry.

36 Castor, *She-Wolves*, 283–96; Gemma Hollman, *The Queen and the Mistress: The Women of Edward III* (Cheltenham, UK: History Press, 2022), 21–25.

37 *Vita Edward Secundi: The Life of Edward the Second*, ed. Wendy R. Childs (Oxford: Clarendon Press, 2005), 243.

38 J. F. Verbruggen, "8 Women in Medieval Armies," *Journal of Medieval Military History* 4 (2006): 129–30; K. E. Sjursen, "Pirate, Traitor, Wife: Jeanne de Belleville and the Categories of Fourteenth-Century French Noblewomen," in *Medieval Elite Women and the Exercise of Power, 1100–1400*, ed. H. J. Tanner (Cham, Switzerland: Palgrave Macmillan, 2019), 135–56.

IV. WRITERS AND ARTISTS

1 Kathleen Palti, "Singing Women: Lullabies and Carols in Medieval England," *Journal of English and Germanic Philology* 110, no. 3 (2011): 359, 363, 374.

2 Joan M. Ferrante, "The French Courtly Poet: Marie de France," in *Medieval Women Writers*, ed. Katharina M. Wilson (Manchester, UK: Manchester University Press, 1984), 64; Peter Dronke, "The Provençal Trobairitz: Castelloza," in *Medieval Women Writers*, ed. Katharina M. Wilson (Manchester, UK: Manchester University Press, 1984), 131.

3 Therese Martin, "Exceptions and Assumptions: Women in Medieval Art History," in *Reassessing the Roles of Women as "Makers" of Medieval Art and Architecture*, ed. Therese Martin (Leiden, Netherlands: Brill, 2015), 2–4.

4 Luke Syson and Dora Thornton, *Objects of Virtue: Art in Renaiossance Italy* (Los Angeles: J. Paul Getty Museum, 2001), 191–92.

5 Ibid., 192–94; Meredith Small, *Inventing the World: Venice and the Transformation of Western Civilization* (New York: Simon and Schuster, 2020).

6 Nancy L. Wicker, "Nimble-Fingered Maidens in Scandinavia: Women as Artists and Patrons," in *Reassessing the Roles of Women as "Makers" of Medieval Art and Architecture*, ed. Therese Martin (Leiden, Netherlands: Brill, 2015), 865–67.

7 Ibid., 869–71, 896.

8 Annemarie Weyl Carr, "Women as Artists in the Middle Ages: 'The Dark Is Light Enough,'" in *Dictionary*

of Women Artists, vol. 1, Introductory Surveys, Artists, A–I, ed. Delia Gaze (London: Fitzroy Dearborn, 1997), 13.

9 Leslie Ross, Artists of the Middle Ages (Westport, CT: Greenwood Press, 2003), 72–73.

10 Stefanie Seeberg, "Women as Makers of Church Decoration: Illustrated Textiles at the Monasteries of Altenberg/Lahn, Rupertsberg, and Heiningen (13th–14th c.)," in Reassessing the Roles of Women as "Makers" of Medieval Art and Architecture, ed. Therese Martin (Leiden, Netherlands: Brill, 2015), 384–85.

11 Jeffrey F. Hamburger, Nuns as Artists: The Visual Culture of a Medieval Convent (Berkeley: University of California Press, 1997), 206–7.

12 Thérèse B. McGuire, "Monastic Artists and Educators of the Middle Ages," Woman's Art Journal 9, no. 2 (1988–89): 3.

13 Steinunn Kristjánsdóttir, "The Abbesses of Iceland," Religions 14, no. 4 (2023): article 533, 9–10.

14 McGuire, "Monastic Artists," 4.

15 Carr, "Women as Artists," 7.

16 Seeberg, "Women as Makers," 357; Ane Preisler Skovgaard, "The Fabric of Devotion: A New Approach to Studying Textiles from Late Medieval Nunneries," Konsthistorisk Tidskrift/ Journal of Art History 90, no. 1 (2021): 46.

17 McGuire, "Monastic Artists," 3–4.

18 Carr, "Women as Artists," 5.

19 Wicker, "Nimble-Fingered Maidens," 890–94.

20 Matilda Tomaryn Bruckner, "Fictions of the Female Voice: The Women Troubadours," Speculum 67, no. 4 (1992): 868.

21 Dronke, "The Provençal Trobairitz," 131; Bruckner, "Fictions of the Female Voice," 870–71.

22 Martha W. Driver, "Medieval Women Writers and What They Read, c. 1100–c. 1500," in The Edinburgh History of Reading: Early Readers, ed. Mary Hammond (Edinburgh: Edinburgh University Press, 2020), 57.

23 Ibid., 56–57.

24 Ferrante, "The French Courtly Poet," 64.

25 Ibid., 64–67; Driver, "Medieval Women Writers," 54, 58–59.

26 Montserrat Piera, Women Readers and Writers in Medieval Iberia: Spinning the Text (Leiden, Netherlands, and Boston: Brill, 2019), 177, 184, 193.

27 Joseph Snow, "The Spanish Love Poet: Florencia Pinar," in Medieval Women Writers, ed. Katharina M. Wilson (Manchester, UK: Manchester

University Press, 1984), 321–24.

28 Piera, Women Readers, 33–35.

29 Jacqueline Broad and Karen Green, A History of Women's Political Thought in Europe, 1400–1700 (Cambridge: Cambridge University Press, 2009), 10; Driver, "Medieval Women Writers," 68; S. H. Rigby, "The Wife of Bath, Christine de Pizan, and the Medieval Case for Women," Chaucer Review 35, no. 2 (2000): 137–49.

30 Dieuwke van der Poel and Hermina Joldersma, "Women's Writing from the Low Countries 1200–1575," in Women's Writing from the Low Countries, 1200–1875: A Bilingual Anthology, ed. Lia van Gemert et al. (Amsterdam: Amsterdam University Press, 2010), 25; Emily A. Holmes, Flesh Made Word: Medieval Women Mystics, Writing, and the Incarnation (Waco, TX: Baylor University Press, 2013), 49–50.

31 Ferrante, "The French Courtly Poet," 65.

32 Driver, "Medieval Women Writers," 55, 63–65.

33 Mercedes Pérez Vidal, "The Corpus Christi Devotion: Gender, Liturgy, and Authority among Dominican Nuns in Castile in the Middle Ages," in "Gender and Status in the Medieval World," special issue, Historical Reflections/Réflexions Historiques 42, no. 1 (2016): 40; Liz Herbert Mcavoy, "'O der lady, be my help'": Women's Visionary Writing and the Devotional Literary Canon," in "Women's Literary Culture and Late Medieval English Writing," special issue, Chaucer Review 51, no. 1 (2016): 69; Carr, "Women as Artists," 11.

34 Sara S. Poor, "'Ich schreyberin': Rethinking Female Authorship with Anna Eybin's Table of Contents," in "Medieval Women's Religious Texts in the Germanic Regions," special issue, Journal of Medieval Religious Cultures 42, no. 2 (2016): 203.

35 Gemma Hollman, The Queen and the Mistress: The Women of Edward III (Cheltenham, UK: History Press, 2022), 61.

36 Broad and Green, A History of Women's Political Thought, 26–29.

37 Albrecht Classen, The Power of a Woman's Voice in Medieval and Early Modern Literatures: New Approaches to German and European Women Writers and to Violence against Women in Premodern Times (Berlin and New York: Walter de Gruyter, 2007), 311–23.

38 Pamela Sheingorn, "'The Wise Mother': The Image of St. Anne Teaching the Virgin Mary," Gesta 32,

no. 1 (1993): 69–71; Susan Schibanoff, "Botticelli's Madonna del Magnificat: Constructing the Woman Writer in Early Humanist Italy," Publications of the Modern Language Association of America 109, no. 2 (1994): 192–93.

39 Schibanoff, "Botticelli's Madonna," 202–3.

40 Broad and Green, A History of Women's Political Thought, 42.

41 Schibanoff, "Botticelli's Madonna," 195.

42 Broad and Green, A History of Women's Political Thought, 44–45.

43 Schibanoff, "Botticelli's Madonna," 201; van der Poel and Joldersma, "Women's Writing," 34.

44 Beach, "Claustration and Collaboration between the Sexes in the Twelfth-Century Scriptorium," 59.

45 Hamburger, Nuns as Artists, 181.

46 Beach, "Claustration and Collaboration," 62–63.

47 Poor, "'Ich schreyberin,'" 204; Cynthia J. Cyrus, The Scribes for Women's Convents in Late Medieval Germany (Toronto: University of Toronto Press, 2009), 25–26.

48 Cyrus, The Scribes, 28; van der Poel and Joldersma, "Women's Writing," 29.

49 Katherine Gill, "Women and the Production of Religious Literature in the Vernacular, 1300–1500," in Creative Women in Medieval and Early Modern Italy: A Religious and Artistic Renaissance, eds. E. Ann Matter and John Coakley (Philadelphia: University of Pennsylvania Press, 1994), 67–68.

50 Poor, "'Ich schreyberin,'" 204–6.

51 Hamburger, Nuns as Artists, 200–201.

52 Gill, "Women and the Production of Religious Literature," 68; Pierre Alain Mariaux, "Women in the Making: Early Medieval Signatures and Artists' Portraits (9th–12th c.)," in Reassessing the Roles of Women as "Makers" of Medieval Art and Architecture, ed. Therese Martin (Leiden, Netherlands: Brill, 2015), 413–14; Loretta Vandi, "'The Woman with the Flower': Social and Artistic Identity in Medieval Italy," Gesta 39, no. 1 (2000): 73.

53 Carr, "Women as Artists," 10.

54 Ibid.

55 Richard Rouse and Mary Rouse, Manuscripts and Their Makers: Commercial Book Producers in Medieval Paris, 1200–1500 (Turnhout, Belgium: Harvey Miller, 2000), 235–42.

56 Ibid., 250.

57 Ibid., 243–44.

58 Ibid., 236.

59 Ibid., 239.

FURTHER READING

ART AND ARTISTS

Adams, Jenny, and Nancy Mason Bradbury, eds. *Medieval Women and Their Objects.* Ann Arbor: University of Michigan Press, 2017.

Almond, Richard. "Femmes Fatale: Iconography and the Courtly Huntress in the Later Middle Ages and Renaissance." In *Deer and People*, edited by Karis Baker, Ruth Carden, and Richard Madgwick, 257–69. Oxford: Oxbow Books, 2014.

Blud, Victoria, Diane Heath, and Einat Klafter, eds. *Gender in Medieval Places, Spaces and Thresholds.* London: University of London Press, 2019.

Carr, Annemarie Weyl. "Women as Artists in the Middle Ages: The Dark Is Light Enough.'" In *Introductory Surveys, Artists, A–I*, edited by Delia Gaze, 3–21. Vol. 1 of *Dictionary of Women Artists.* London: Fitzroy Dearborn Publishers,

1997.Fitzroy Dearborn Publishers, 1997.

Hamburger, Jeffrey F. Nuns as Artists: The Visual Culture *of a Medieval Convent.* Berkeley: University of California Press, 1997.

Lillich, Meredith Parsons. "Gothic Glaziers: Monks, Jews, Taxpayers, Bretons, Women." *Journal of Glass Studies* 27 (1985): 72–92.

Martin, Therese, ed. *Reassessing the Roles of Women as "Makers" of Medieval Art and Architecture.* Leiden, Netherlands: Brill, 2015.

Matter, E. Ann, and John Coakley, eds. *Creative Women in Medieval and Early Modern Italy: A Religious and Artistic Renaissance.* Philadelphia: University of Pennsylvania Press, 1994.

McGuire, Thérèse B. "Monastic Artists and Educators of the Middle Ages." *Woman's*

Art Journal 9, no. 2 (1988–89): 3–9.

Ross, Leslie. *Artists of the Middle Ages.* Westport, CT: Greenwood Press, 2003.

Rouse, Richard, and Mary Rouse. *Manuscripts and Their Makers: Commercial Book Producers in Medieval Paris, 1200–1500.* Turnhout, Belgium: Harvey Miller, 2000.

Sheingorn, Pamela. "'The Wise Mother': The Image of St. Anne Teaching the Virgin Mary." *Gesta* 32, no. 1 (1993): 69–80.

Syson, Luke, and Dora Thornton. *Objects of Virtue: Art in Renaissance Italy.* Los Angeles: J. Paul Getty Museum, 2001.

Vandi, Loretta. "'The Woman with the Flower': Social and Artistic Identity in Medieval Italy." *Gesta* 39, no. 1 (2000): 73–77.

LITERATURE

The Ballad of the Tyrannical Husband. Translated by Jeremy Goldberg, 2002. University of York. https://www.york.ac.uk/teaching/ history/pjpg/BALLAD.htm.

Bruckner, Matilda Tomaryn. "Fictions of the Female Voice: The Women Troubadours." *Speculum* 67, no. 4 (1992): 865–91.

Cabré, Montserrat. "From a Master to a Laywoman: A Feminine Manual of Self-Help." *Dynamis: Acta Hispanica ad Medicinae Scientiarumque Historiam Illustrandam* 20 (2000): 371–93.

Castellví, Francesc de, Bernat Fenollar, and Narcís Vinyoles. *Scachs d'Amor.* Translated by Josep Miquel Sobrer, n.d. https://www.scachsdamor.org/.

Classen, Albrecht. *The Power of a Woman's Voice in Medieval and Early Modern Literatures: New Approaches to German and European Women Writers and to Violence against Women in Premodern Times.* Berlin and New York: Walter de Gruyter, 2007.

Driver, Martha W. "Medieval Women Writers and What They Read, c. 1100–c. 1500." In *The Edinburgh History of Reading: Early Readers*, edited by Mary Hammond, 54–73. Edinburgh: Edinburgh University Press, 2020.

The Goodman of Paris (Le Ménagier

de Paris): A Treatise on Moral and Domestic Economy by a Citizen of Paris, c. 1393. Translated by Eileen Power. Woodbridge, UK: Boydell Press, 2006.

Hindsley, Leonard P. *The Mystics of Engelthal: Writings from a Medieval Monastery.* New York: St. Martin's Press, 1998.

Holmes, Emily A. *Flesh Made Word: Medieval Women Mystics, Writing, and the Incarnation.* Waco, TX: Baylor University Press, 2013.

Juel, Kristin. "Chess, Love, and the Rhetoric of Distraction in Medieval French Narrative." *Romance Philology* 64, no. 1 (2010): 73–97.

La Tour-Landry, Geoffroy de. *The Book of the Knight of La Tour-Landry*, edited by Thomas Wright. London: Kegan Paul, Trench, Trubner, 1906.

Mcavoy, Liz Herbert. "'O der lady, be my help': Women's Visionary Writing and the Devotional Literary Canon." In "Women's Literary Culture and Late Medieval English Writing." Special issue, *Chaucer Review* 51, no. 1 (2016): 68–87.

"Medieval Women's Religious Texts in the Germanic Regions." Special issue, *Journal of Medieval Religious Cultures* 42, no. 2 (2016).

Palti, Kathleen. "Singing Women: Lullabies and Carols in Medieval England." *Journal of English and Germanic Philology* 110, no. 3 (2011): 359–82.

Piera, Montserrat. *Women Readers and Writers in Medieval Iberia: Spinning the Text.* Leiden, Netherlands, and Boston: Brill, 2019.

Pisan, Christine de. *The Treasure of the City of Ladies.* Translated by Sarah Lawson. London: Penguin Books, 1985.

Rigby, S. H. "The Wife of Bath, Christine de Pizan, and the Medieval Case for Women." *Chaucer Review* 35, no. 2 (2000): 133–65.

Schibanoff, Susan. "Botticelli's *Madonna del Magnificat*: Constructing the Woman Writer in Early Humanist Italy." *Publications of the Modern Language Association of America* 109, no. 2 (1994): 190–206.

Strohm, Paul. *Hochon's Arrow: The Social Imagination of Fourteenth-Century Texts.* Princeton, NJ: Princeton University Press, 1992.

van der Poel, Dieuwke, and Hermina Joldersma. "Women's Writing from the Low Countries, 1200–1575." In *Women's Writing from the Low Countries, 1200–1875: A Bilingual Anthology*, edited by Lia van Gemert et al., 21–38. Amsterdam: Amsterdam University Press, 2010.

Wilson, Katharina M., ed. *Medieval Women Writers.* Manchester, UK: Manchester University Press, 1984.

RELIGIOUS WOMEN

Barstow, Anne Llewellyn. "Joan of Arc and Female Mysticism." *Journal of Feminist Studies in Religion* 1, no. 2 (1985): 29–42.

Berman, Constance Hoffman. *The White Nuns: Cistercian Abbeys for Women in Medieval France.* Philadelphia: University of Pennsylvania Press, 2018.

Clark, Katherine. "Purgatory, Punishment, and the Discourse of Holy Widowhood in the High and Later Middle Ages." *Journal of the History of Sexuality* 16, no. 2 (2007): 169–203.

Cyrus, Cynthia J. *The Scribes for Women's*

Convents in Late Medieval Germany. Toronto: University of Toronto Press, 2009.

Evangelisti, Silvia. "'We Do Not Have It, and We Do Not Want It': Women, Power, and Convent Reform in Florence." *Sixteenth Century Journal* 34, no. 3 (2003): 677–700.

Fanous, Samuel, and Henrietta Leyser, eds. *Christina of Markyate: A Twelfth-Century Holy Woman.* Oxford: Routledge, 2005.

Farmer, Sharon, and Barbara Rosenwein, eds. *Monks and Nuns, Saints and Outcasts.* Ithaca, NY, and London: Cornell University Press, 2000.

Flanagan, Sabina. *Hildegard of Bingen: A Visionary Life.* London: Routledge, 1998.

Freed, John B. *Noble Bondsmen: Ministerial Marriages in the Archdiocese of Salzburg, 1100–1343.* Ithaca, NY, and London: Cornell University Press, 1995.

Gregory, Rabia. "Thinking of Their Sisters: Authority and Authorship in Late Medieval Women's Religious Communities." *Journal of Medieval Religious Cultures* 40, no. 1 (2014): 75–100.

Izbicki, Thomas M. "Nuns' Clothing and Ornaments in English and Northern

by Gale R. Owen-Crocker and Maren Clegg Hyer, 237–54. Woodbridge, UK: Boydell and Brewer, 2019.

Johnson, Penelope. *Equal in Monastic Profession: Religious Women in Medieval France*. Chicago: University of Chicago Press, 1991.

Kristjánsdóttir, Steinunn. "The Abbesses of Iceland." *Religions* 14, no. 4 (2023): article 533.

Oliva, Marilyn. "Counting Nuns: A Prosopography of Late Medieval English Nuns in the Diocese of Norwich." In "The Late Medieval English Church." Special issue, *Medieval Prosopography* 16, no. 1, (1995): 27–55.

Vidal, Mercedes Pérez. "The Corpus Christi Devotion: Gender, Liturgy, and Authority among Dominican Nuns in Castile in the Middle Ages." In "Gender and Status in the Medieval World." Special issue, *Historical Reflections/Réflexions Historiques* 42, no. 1 (2016): 35–47.

ROYALTY

Baldwin, David. *Elizabeth Woodville: Mother of the Princes in the Tower*. Stroud, UK: Sutton, 2002.

Brzezińska, Anna. "Jadwiga of Anjou as the Image of a Good Queen in Late Medieval and Early Modern Poland." *Polish Review* 44, no. 4 (1999): 407–18.

Castor, Helen. *She-Wolves: The Women Who Ruled England before Elizabeth*. London: Faber and Faber, 2011.

Cockerill, Sara. *Eleanor of Castile: The Shadow Queen*. Stroud, UK: Amberley, 2015.

Etting, Vivian. *Queen Margrete I (1353–1412) and the Founding of the Nordic Union*. Leiden, Netherlands, and Boston: Brill, 2004.

Hollman, Gemma. *The Queen and the Mistress: The Women of Edward III*. Cheltenham, UK: History Press, 2022.

———. *Royal Witches: From Joan of Navarre to Elizabeth Woodville*. Cheltenham, UK: History Press, 2019.

Knoll, Paul W. "Jadwiga and Education." *Polish Review* 44, no. 4 (1999): 419–32.

Lee, Patricia-Ann. "Reflections of Power: Margaret of Anjou and the Dark Side of Queenship." *Renaissance Quarterly* 39, no. 2 (1986): 183–217.

Magna Carta, 1215. Translated by the British Library. National Archives, UK. https://www.nationalarchives.gov.uk/education/resources/magna-carta/british-library-magna-carta-1215-runnymede/.

Maurer, Helen E. *Margaret of Anjou: Queenship and Power in Late Medieval England*. Woodbridge, UK: Boydell Press, 2003.

Ormrod, Mark. "The Royal Nursery: A Household for the Younger Children of Edward III." *English Historical Review* 120, no. 486 (2005): 398–415.

Sekules, Veronica. "Dynasty and Patrimony in the Self-Construction of an English Queen: Philippa of Hainault and Her Images." In *England and the Continent in the Middle Ages: Proceedings of the 1996 Harlaxton Symposium*, Harlaxton Medieval Studies 8, edited by John Mitchell and Matthew Moran, 157–74. Stamford, UK: Shaun Tyas, 2000.

Shenton, Caroline. "Philippa of Hainault's Churchings: The Politics of Motherhood at the Court of Edward III." In *Family and Dynasty: Proceedings of the 1997 Harlaxton Symposium*, Harlaxton Medieval Studies 9, edited by Richard Eales and Shaun Tyas, 105–21. Donington, UK: Shaun Tyas, 2003.

Turner, Ralph V. *Eleanor of Aquitaine: Queen of France, Queen of England*. New Haven, CT: Yale University Press, 2009.

Vita Edward Secundi: The Life of Edward the Second, edited by Wendy R. Childs. Oxford: Clarendon Press, 2005.

SOCIAL HISTORY

Borrero Fernández, Mercedes. "Peasant and Aristocratic Women: Their Role and the Rural Economy of Seville at the End of the Middle Ages." In *Women at Work in Spain: From the Middle Ages to Early Modern Times*, edited by Marilyn Stone and Carmen Benito-Vessels, 11–32. New York: Peter Lang, 1998.

Britnell, R. H. "Specialization of Work in England, 1100–1300." *Economic History Review* 54, no. 1 (2001): 1–16.

Broad, Jacqueline, and Karen Green. *A History of Women's Political Thought in Europe, 1400–1700*. Cambridge: Cambridge University Press, 2009.

Cabré, Montserrat. "Women or Healers? Household Practices and the Categories of Health Care in Late Medieval Iberia." In "Women, Health, and Healing in Early Modern Europe." Special issue, *Bulletin of the History of Medicine* 82, no. 1 (2008): 18–51.

Dincer, Aysu. "Wills, Marriage and Business Contracts: Urban Women in Late-Medieval Cyprus." *Gender and History* 24, no. 2 (2012): 310–32.

"Dunbar, Agnes, Countess of Dunbar and March." *Oxford Dictionary of National Biography*. Oxford: Oxford University Press, online. https://doi.org/10.1093/odnb/9780192683120.013.8200.

Dyer, Christopher. "The Material World of English Peasants, 1200–1540: Archaeological Perspectives on Rural Economy and Welfare." *Agricultural History Review* 62, no. 1 (2014): 1–22.

Earenfight, Theresa, ed. *Women and Wealth in Late Medieval Europe*. New York: Palgrave Macmillan, 2010.

Goldberg, Jeremy. *Women, Work, and Life Cycle in a Medieval Economy: Women in York and Yorkshire c. 1300–1520*. Oxford: Clarendon Press, 1992.

Hanawalt, Barbara A. "Medieval English Women in Rural and Urban Domestic Space." *Dumbarton Oaks Papers* 52 (1998): 19–26.

Herlihy, David. *Opera Muliebria: Women and Work in Medieval Europe*. New York and London: McGraw-Hill, 1990.

Howell, Martha C. *Women, Production, and Patriarchy in Late Medieval Cities*. Chicago: University of Chicago Press, 1986.

Leyser, Henrietta. *Medieval Women: A Social History of Women in England 450–1500*. London: Phoenix Press, 2002.

Lochrie, Karma. *Heterosyncrasies: Female Sexuality When Normal Wasn't*. Minneapolis: University of Minnesota Press, 2005.

McCarthy, Caley. "The Valuation of Care Work: Wet Nurses at the Hôpital du Saint-Esprit in Marseille." In "Gender and the History of Care Work." *Clio: Women, Gender, History*, no. 49 (2019): 45–67.

Murray, James M. *Bruges, Cradle of Capitalism, 1280–1390*. Cambridge: Cambridge University Press, 2005.

New, Elizabeth A., and Christian Steer, eds. *Medieval Londoners: Essays to Mark the Eightieth Birthday of Caroline M. Barron*. London: University of London Press, 2019.

Parsons, John Carmi. "The Pregnant Queen as Counsellor and the Medieval Construction of Motherhood." In *Medieval Mothering*, edited by John Carmi Parsons and Bonnie Wheeler, 39–62. New York and London: Garland, 1996.

Phillips, Kim M. *Medieval Maidens: Young Women and Gender in England, 1270–1540*. Manchester, UK: Manchester University Press, 2003.

Pierce, Joanne M. "'Green Women' and Blood Pollution: Some Medieval Rituals for the Churching of Women after Childbirth." *Studia Liturgica* 29, no. 2 (1999): 191–215.

Sjursen, K. E. "Pirate, Traitor, Wife: Jeanne de Belleville and the Categories of Fourteenth-Century French Noblewomen." In *Medieval Elite Women and the Exercise of Power, 1100–1400*, edited by H. J. Tanner, 135–56. Cham, Switzerland: Palgrave Macmillan, 2019.

Small, Meredith. *Inventing the World: Venice and the Transformation of Western Civilization*. New York: Simon and Schuster, 2020.

Spencer, Charles. *The White Ship: Conquest, Anarchy and the Wrecking of Henry I's Dream*. London: Harper Collins, 2021.

Stöber, Karen. "Female Patrons of Late Medieval English Monasteries." *Medieval Prosopography* 31 (2016): 115–36.

Stow, John. *Annals of England to 1603*. N.p., c. 1603.

Swabey, Ffiona. *Medieval Gentlewoman: Life in a Widow's Household in the Later Middle Ages*. Stroud, UK: Sutton, 1999.

Verbruggen, J. F. "8 Women in Medieval Armies." *Journal of Medieval Military History* 4 (2006): 119–36.

Whittle, Jane. "Housewives and Servants in Rural England, 1440–1650: Evidence of Women's Work from Probate Documents." *Transactions of the Royal Historical Society* 15 (2005): 51–74.

Woolgar, C. M., D. Serjeantson, and T. Waldron, eds. *Food in Medieval England: Diet and Nutrition*. Oxford: Oxford University Press, 2006.

"Working Together in the Middle Ages: Perspectives on Women's Communities." *Signs: Journal of Women in Culture and Society* 14, no. 2 (1989).

INDEX

PHOTOGRAPHY CREDITS